Dissertation Discovery Company and University of Florida are dedicated to making scholarly works more discoverable and accessible throughout the world.

This dissertation, "A Multiscale Spline Derivative-based Transform for Image Fusion and Enhancement" by Iztok Koren, was obtained from University of Florida and is being sold with permission from the author. The content of this dissertation has not been altered in any way. We have altered the formatting in order to facilitate the ease of printing and reading of the dissertation.

Mojim staršem

ACKNOWLEDGEMENTS

I would like to thank my mentors Dr. Fred J. Taylor and Dr. Andrew F. Laine for their help and support. They gave me the freedom to explore research directions that interested me most and provided me with the excellent work environment.

I am grateful to Dr. Jose C. Principe, Dr. John M. M. Anderson, and Dr. Kermit Sigmon for serving on my committee and for their comments on my dissertation.

I would also like to thank all the members of the High Speed Digital Architecture Laboratory and the Image Processing Research Group for their friendship and help.

Last but not least, I want to thank my family for their support and understanding, and for bearing with me when I was unbearable.

TABLE OF CONTENTS

LIST OF TABLES

LIST OF FIGURES

Abstract of Dissertation Presented to the Graduate School
of the University of Florida in Partial Fulfillment of the
Requirements for the Degree of Doctor of Philosophy

A MULTISCALE SPLINE DERIVATIVE-BASED TRANSFORM
FOR IMAGE FUSION AND ENHANCEMENT

By

Iztok Koren

December 1996

Chairman: Dr. Fred J. Taylor
Cochairman: Dr. Andrew F. Laine
Major Department: Electrical and Computer Engineering

Analyzing images along distinct scales is advantageous in many image processing and computational vision tasks. Traditional wavelet transforms have become
a popular tool for multiscale image analysis and image compression suffer from artifacts, lack shift and rotation invariance, and may introduce aliasing and anisotropies.
We propose a highly redundant representation that eliminates these artifacts.

A new transform is constructed as an extension of the discrete dyadic wavelet
transform with a wavelet being the first derivative of a central B-spline. We begin
the construction in one dimension by providing an efficient initialization procedure
for the computation of the discrete dyadic wavelet transform and by extending the
transform to encompass higher order derivatives.

This modified one-dimensional discrete dyadic wavelet transform will serve
as a basis for deriving a steerable two-dimensional transform. Such a transform is

advantageous in that it does not introduce any of the artifacts described above. However, exact reconstruction is problematic via implementation in the spatial domain. We solve this problem by devising a spline-based approximation. The resulting algorithm for computing a multiscale spline derivative-based transform is implemented efficiently as a filter bank consisting of separable filters alone. For both finite and infinite impulse response filters present in the filter bank, we specify implementation details of a realization that alleviates the boundary effects caused by the use of circular convolution.

Finally, we use the derived transform for multiscale image fusion and enhancement. We show empirically that the transform does not introduce artifacts commonly reported for traditional wavelet-based implementations and provides more flexibility for different fusion and enhancement strategies by enabling orientation analysis.

CHAPTER 1
INTRODUCTION

Analyzing images across multiple scales and resolution has become a powerful tool for solving compelling problems in computational vision, image processing, and pattern recognition. Wavelet theory encompasses multiscale and multiresolution representations, such as subband filtering [40], image pyramids [4], and scale space filtering [48], into a unified mathematical framework. In the area of image processing, there remain few research areas to which wavelet analysis has not been applied. For example, problems in image compression, denoising, restoration, enhancement, registration, fusion, segmentation, and analysis, have all been approached with distinct kinds of wavelet processing.

Though ubiquitous, wavelet analysis is not without problems of its own. Lack of translation invariance, one of the major problems of the wavelet transform [10], is in multiple dimensions accompanied with lack of rotation invariance.

1.1 Shortcomings of Traditional Methods of Wavelet Analysis

A wavelet transform in its most commonly used orthogonal or biorthogonal forms is not translation and rotation-invariant. By translation-invariant transform, we mean a transform that commutes with a translation operator. Since we will deal primarily with discrete transforms in this work, we constrain the translation parameter to integer multiples of a sampling period.

Lack of translation invariance of the discrete wavelet transform is illustrated in Figure 1.1. Here, we can clearly see how a translation of the input signal by one

1

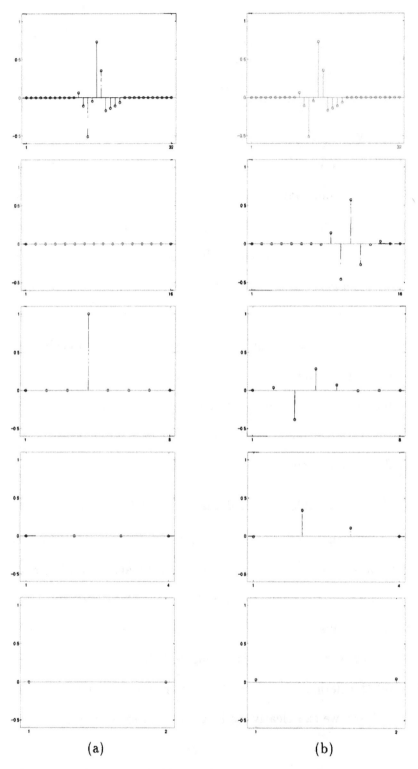

Figure 1.1: (a) Original signal and (b) signal translated one sample to the left with its discrete wavelet transform coefficients shown across dyadic scales 2^m, $m \in \{1, 2, 3, 4\}$.

sample results in a completely different set of transform coefficients (orthogonal wavelet DAUB4[1] [10] was used in this experiment).

Noninvariance under translations of an orthogonal and biorthogonal wavelet transform is due to lower sampling density at coarser scales.[2] A straightforward way of dealing with this problem is to construct a redundant transform by using the same sampling frequency for the input signal and all scales of the transform. A filter bank implementation of such a transform, called "algorithme à trous" [15], is based upon the fact that downsampling followed by filtering is equivalent to filtering with the upsampled filter before the downsampling, as shown in Figure 1.2.

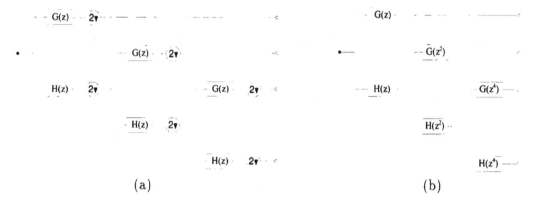

(a)   (b)

Figure 1.2: Filter bank implementation for (a) a discrete wavelet transform and (b) "algorithme à trous" decompositions for three levels of analysis.

Lack of rotation invariance is another shortcoming of traditional (i.e., orthogonal and biorthogonal) wavelet techniques. In defining rotation invariance, we are a bit less strict than with translation invariance. We do not require that the transform commutes with a rotation operator here. Even in the case of a simple filtering, this would limit us to circularly symmetric filters only. Our requirement for analysis is a

---

[1]The number in DAUB4 refers to twice the order of the wavelet (i.e., two in this case).

[2]In practice, since analysis is performed over a finite range of scales, a discrete wavelet transform is translation-invariant by translations determined by the coarsest scale (e.g., sixteen samples for the analysis from Figure 1.1) [10].

transform that enables rotation-invariant processing. As an example of such a transform, let us consider filtering with the first derivative of a two-dimensional Gaussian probability density function in two directions, specifically, along x and along y-axis. By linearly combining the results of filtering in these two directions, filtering with the first derivative of a Gaussian in any direction can be computed. This fact was used by Canny [6] for edge detection. A determined edge direction rotates as an input image is rotated.

After choosing the fundamental properties of the transform, one must decide upon the basis functions to be applied. For our studies, we selected basis functions that well approximated derivatives of a Gaussian, because (1) the Gaussian probability density function is optimally concentrated in both time and frequency domain, and thus suitable for time-frequency analysis, (2) higher order derivatives of a Gaussian can be, similar to the first derivative, used for rotation-invariant processing [12], and (3) the Gaussian function generates a causal (in a sense that a coarse scale depends exclusively on the previous finer scale) scale space [2]. The last property makes possible scale-space "tracking" of emergent features.

1.2 Thesis Overview

We wish to construct an invertible, translation and rotation-invariant two-dimensional transform that decomposes an image using a set of basis functions which are approximations to derivatives of the Gaussian probability density function.

To obtain a translation-invariant representation, we will use "algorithme à trous," or more precisely, we will extend the discrete dyadic wavelet transform [28], which uses "algorithme à trous." Derivatives of a Gaussian will be approximated by wavelets which are derivatives of central B-spline functions. In Chapter 2, we review the basics of B-spline processing necessary to derive transforms in later chapters.

Next, Chapter 3 examines a dyadic wavelet transform in one dimension. We present extensions of the discrete dyadic wavelet transform to higher order derivatives and to even order spline functions. To compute a discrete transform from a continuous one, the discrete computation must be properly initialized. We devise a new initialization procedure that is shown to be more accurate than the one suggested by Mallat and Zhong [28]. After the derivation of the transform, we point out relevant connections to scale-space filtering and reconstruction from edges.

In case of the first derivative of a Gaussian, a rotation-invariant transform can be obtained by a tensor product extension of the one-dimensional transform to two dimensions. For second order derivatives, a tensor product approach can approximate Laplacian of a Gaussian, but cannot perform orientation analysis (due to its isotropic nature). In Chapter 4, we first examine the above two cases, and then develop a new multiscale spline derivative-based transform, which in addition enables rotation-invariant processing for derivatives of orders higher than two.

Given that the developed transform is highly redundant, an efficient implementation is extremely advantageous. This issue is addressed in Chapter 5. When filtering of a signal is performed by circular convolution, boundary effects may result. A standard way of dealing with this problem is by mirror-extending the input signal to the filter. We combine such an extension with symmetry/antisymmetry of the filters, to achieve savings in both computation time and memory.

Finally, in Chapter 6, we present two sample applications: image fusion and enhancement. We demonstrate that the new transform does not cause artifacts commonly associated with traditional wavelet techniques and is an attractive analytic tool for designing novel fusion and enhancement strategies.

1.3 Notation

We use symbols N, Z, and R for the sets of naturals, integers, and reals, respectively.

$L^2(R)$ and $L^2(R^2)$ denote the Hilbert spaces of measurable, square-integrable functions $f(x)$ and $f(x,y)$, respectively.

The inner product of two functions $f(x) \in L^2(\mathbf{R})$ and $g(x) \in L^2(\mathbf{R})$ is given by

$$\langle f(x), g(x) \rangle = \int_{-\infty}^{\infty} f(x)\, g(x)\, dx.$$

The norm of a function $f(x) \in L^2(\mathbf{R})$ is defined as

$$\|f\| = \sqrt{\int_{-\infty}^{\infty} |f(x)|^2\, dx}.$$

The convolution of functions $f(x) \in L^2(\mathbf{R})$ and $g(x) \in L^2(\mathbf{R})$ is computed as

$$f * g(x) = \int_{-\infty}^{\infty} f(t)\, g(x-t)\, dt,$$

and the convolution of two functions $f(x,y) \in L^2(\mathbf{R}^2)$ and $g(x,y) \in L^2(\mathbf{R}^2)$ equals

$$f * g(x,y) = \int_{-\infty}^{\infty} \int_{-\infty}^{\infty} f(t_x, t_y)\, g(x - t_x, y - t_y)\, dt_x\, dt_y.$$

The Fourier transform of a function $f(x) \in L^2(\mathbf{R})$ is defined as

$$\hat{f}(\omega) = \int_{-\infty}^{\infty} f(x) e^{-j\omega x}\, dx,$$

and the Fourier transform of a function $f(x,y) \in L^2(\mathbf{R}^2)$ is equal to

$$\hat{f}(\omega_x, \omega_y) = \int_{-\infty}^{\infty} \int_{-\infty}^{\infty} f(x,y) e^{-j(\omega_x x + \omega_y y)}\, dx\, dy.$$

$l^2(\mathbf{Z})$ and $l^2(\mathbf{Z}^2)$ stand for the spaces of square-summable discrete signals $f(n)$ and $f(n_x, n_y)$, respectively.

The z-transform of a discrete signal $f(n) \in l^2(\mathbf{Z})$ is defined as

$$F(z) = \sum_{n=-\infty}^{\infty} f(n) z^{-n}.$$

The convolution of discrete signals $f(n) \in l^2(\mathbf{Z})$ and $g(n) \in l^2(\mathbf{Z})$ is equal to

$$f * g(n) = \sum_{m=-\infty}^{\infty} f(m)\, g(n-m),$$

and the convolution of discrete signals $f(n_x, n_y) \in l^2(\mathbf{Z}^2)$ and $g(n_x, n_y) \in l^2(\mathbf{Z}^2)$ is given by

$$f * g(n_x, n_y) = \sum_{m_x=-\infty}^{\infty} \sum_{m_y=-\infty}^{\infty} f(m_x, m_y)\, g(n_x - m_x, n_y - m_y).$$

The Fourier transform of a discrete signal $f(n) \in l^2(\mathbf{Z})$ is equal to the z-transform evaluated on the unit circle

$$F(\omega) = \sum_{n=-\infty}^{\infty} f(n) e^{-j\omega n},$$

and the Fourier transform of a discrete signal $f(n_x, n_y) \in l^2(\mathbf{Z}^2)$ is defined as

$$F(\omega_x, \omega_y) = \sum_{n_x=-\infty}^{\infty} \sum_{n_y=-\infty}^{\infty} f(n_x, n_y) e^{-j(\omega_x n_x + \omega_y n_y)}.$$

For later use, we define the following functions:

1. the unit impulse function

$$\delta_u(x) := \begin{cases} 1 & \text{for } x = 0 \\ 0 & \text{otherwise,} \end{cases}$$

2. the unit step function

$$u(x) := \begin{cases} 1 & \text{for } x \geq 0 \\ 0 & \text{for } x < 0, \end{cases}$$

3. the rectangular function

$$\text{rect}(x) := \begin{cases} 1 & \text{for } |x| \leq \frac{1}{2} \\ 0 & \text{for } |x| > \frac{1}{2}, \end{cases}$$

4. the sinc function

$$\text{sinc}(x) := \frac{\sin(\pi x)}{\pi x}, \quad \text{and}$$

5. the unit impulse sequence

$$\delta(n) := \begin{cases} 1 & \text{for } n = 0 \\ 0 & \text{otherwise,} \end{cases}$$

where $x \in \mathbf{R}$ and $n \in \mathbf{Z}$.

CHAPTER 2
SIGNAL PROCESSING USING CENTRAL B-SPLINES

In this chapter we briefly review fundamentals of spline processing needed for derivations in Chapters 3 and 4.

2.1   Central B-Splines: Definition and Properties

Given real numbers $-\infty \leq x_0 < x_1 < x_2 < \ldots < x_m < x_{m+1} \leq \infty$, a function on the interval $[x_0, x_{m+1}]$ is called a spline function of order p with the knot (i.e., grid point) sequence $x_1, x_2, \ldots x_m$, if it is (1) a polynomial of degree p or less in each interval $[x_i, x_{i+1}]$, $i = 0, 1, \ldots m$, and (2) continuous in its derivatives up to the order $p-1$ on the interval $[x_0, x_{m+1}]$ (i.e., $C^{p-1}[x_0, x_{m+1}]$).

Here, we will concentrate primarily on basis splines (B-splines), or more precisely, central B-splines having knots at $i \in \mathbf{Z}$ for p odd and at $i + \frac{1}{2}$ for p even [34]. Central B-splines of order p (with $p+1$ knots) are defined as

$$\beta_p(x) := \frac{1}{p!} \sum_{i=0}^{p+1} (-1)^i \binom{p+1}{i} \left(x + \frac{p+1}{2} - i\right)^p u\left(x + \frac{p+1}{2} - i\right).$$

Figure 2.1 shows $\beta_p(x)$ and their Fourier transforms $\hat{\beta}_p(\omega)$ for $p \in \{0, 1, 2, 3, 4\}$.

A family of functions $\{\beta_p(x - m)\}_{m \in \mathbf{Z}}$ forms a basis of $\mathbf{S}^p$, a space of order p spline functions with knots at i for p odd and at $i + \frac{1}{2}$ for p even ($i \in \mathbf{Z}$) [34, 35]. Except for $p = 0$, the basis functions $\{\beta_p(x - m)\}$ are not orthogonal.

Let us list some properties of functions $\beta_p(x)$ [3, 34]:

1. $\beta_p(x)$ are nonnegative functions with a support of length $p+1$,

2. $\beta_p(x) = \overbrace{\beta_0 * \beta_0 * \cdots * \beta_0(x)}^{p+1 \text{ times}}$, where "$*$" denotes the convolution operator, or, equivalently, in the Fourier domain:

$$\hat{\beta}_p(\omega) = \left(\frac{\sin(\frac{\omega}{2})}{\frac{\omega}{2}} \right)^{p+1},$$

3. $\beta_p(x) = \frac{1}{p} \left(\left(\frac{p+1}{2} + x \right) \beta_{p-1} \left(x + \frac{1}{2} \right) + \left(\frac{p+1}{2} - x \right) \beta_{p-1} \left(x - \frac{1}{2} \right) \right),$

4. $\frac{\partial \beta_p(x)}{\partial x} = \beta_{p-1} \left(x + \frac{1}{2} \right) - \beta_{p-1} \left(x - \frac{1}{2} \right).$

Another interesting property of B-splines is the fact that they converge to a Gaussian as their order tends to infinity. Unser *et al.* [44] derived the Gaussian approximation

$$\beta_p(x) \simeq \frac{1}{\sqrt{2\pi}\sigma_p} e^{-\frac{x^2}{2\sigma_p^2}},$$

where $\sigma_p = \sqrt{\frac{p+1}{12}}$. Ratio $\frac{\|\beta_p - \tilde{\beta}_p\|^2}{\|\beta_p\|^2}$, for example, is already well below 0.2%.

Denoting by S_1^p a spline function space spanned by $\{\beta_p(x - m)\}$ for p odd and by $\{\beta_p(x - \frac{1}{2} - m)\}$ for p even (subscript in S_1^p refers to the fact that spline functions have knots at integers), spline spaces form a nested sequence $\ldots \subset S_{2^i}^p \subset \ldots \subset S_2^p \subset S_1^p \subset S_{2^{-1}}^p \subset \ldots \subset S_{2^{-i}}^p \subset \ldots$. By orthogonalizing this basis functions a multiresolution analysis of $L^2(\mathbf{R})$, from which the Battle-Lemarié wavelet bases stem, can be built [10]. Here, we will not pursue constructions of orthogonal, semi-orthogonal, or biorthogonal spline-wavelets any further—reader looking for a detailed treatment of this subject may find a good starting point in books [8, 9].

2.2   B-Spline Signal Interpolations

Unser *et al.* developed a fast digital filtering scheme for B-spline signal processing [43]. They defined a discrete B-spline of order p and expansion factor (spacing between knots) m as

$$b_{p,m}(n) := \beta_p \left(\frac{n}{m} \right), \qquad n, m \in \mathbf{Z}.$$

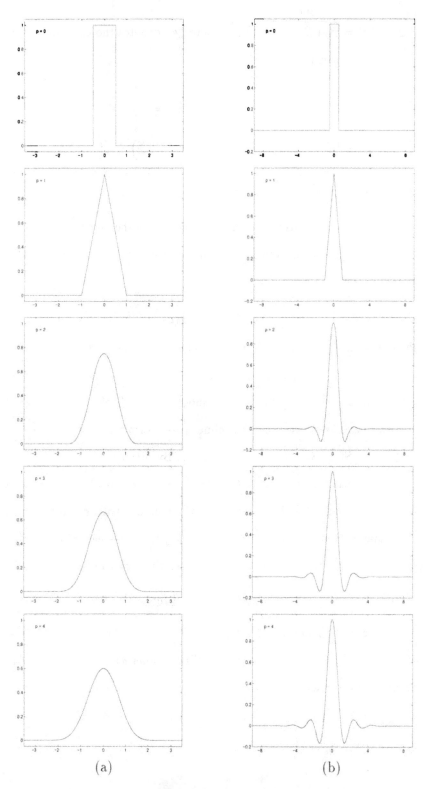

Figure 2.1: Spline functions (a) $\beta_p(x)$ and (b) $\eta_p(x)$ for $p \in \{0, 1, 2, 3, 4\}$.

Henceforth, if the distance between knots equals one, we will write $b_p(n)$ instead of $b_{p,1}(n)$.

Interpolation of a discrete signal $s(n) \in l^2(\mathbf{Z})$ by $s_p(x) \in \mathbf{S}^p$ using central B-splines

$$s(n) = s_p(x)\bigg|_{x=n} = \sum_{i=-\infty}^{\infty} c(i)\beta_p(x-i)\bigg|_{x=n}, \qquad (2.1)$$

can now be written as a convolution sum

$$s(n) = c * b_p(n). \qquad (2.2)$$

If $s(n)$ are samples of a function $s(x)$ bandlimited to $[-\pi, \pi]$ (i.e., the support of its Fourier transform $S(\omega)$ is in $[-\pi, \pi]$), it can be shown that $s_p(x) \to s(x)$ as $p \to \infty$ [1, 36].

In [43], they refer to a linear operator by which B-spline coefficients $c(n)$ can be obtained from samples $s(n)$ as a "direct B-spline transform." Equation (2.2) therefore represents "indirect B-spline transform" of a sequence $\{c(n)\}$.

After taking the z-transform of (2.2), the direct B-spline filters are found to be $b_p^{-1}(n) = \mathcal{Z}^{-1}\{[B_p(z)]^{-1}\}$. Since B-spline functions $\beta_p(x)$ are compactly supported, indirect B-spline filters $b_p(n)$ are finite impulse response (FIR) filters, while direct B-spline filters $b_p^{-1}(n)$ are infinite impulse response (IIR) filters. Aldroubi *et al.* [1] showed that IIR filters $b_p^{-1}(n)$ are stable (i.e., the region of convergence of $B_p^{-1}(z)$ includes the unit circle [30]) for any order p. Note that both indirect and direct B-spline filters are symmetric, which follows from the fact that central B-splines $\beta_p(x)$ are symmetric.

Table 2.1 shows the z-transforms of direct B-spline filters for the first ten orders. We postpone the discussion on implementation details of B-spline filters until Chapter 5.

Table 2.1: Transfer functions of direct B-spline filters for orders from 0 to 9.

p	$B_p^{-1}(z)$
0	1
1	1
2	$\dfrac{8}{z+6+z^{-1}}$
3	$\dfrac{6}{z+4+z^{-1}}$
4	$\dfrac{384}{z^2+76z+230+76z^{-1}+z^{-2}}$
5	$\dfrac{120}{z^2+26z+66+26z^{-1}+z^{-2}}$
6	$\dfrac{46080}{z^3+722z^2+10543z+23548+10543z^{-1}+722z^{-2}+z^{-3}}$
7	$\dfrac{5040}{z^3+120z^2+1191z+2416+1191z^{-1}+120z^{-2}+z^{-3}}$
8	$\dfrac{10321920}{z^4+6552z^3+331612z^2+2485288z+4675014+2485288z^{-1}+331612z^{-2}+6552z^{-3}+z^{-4}}$
9	$\dfrac{362880}{z^4+502z^3+14608z^2+88234z+156190+88234z^{-1}+14608z^{-2}+502z^{-3}+z^{-4}}$

Instead of using B-spline interpolation as given by (2.1) it is sometimes convenient to express the interpolating function $s_p(x)$ in terms of discrete samples $s(n)$

$$s_p(x) = \sum_{i=-\infty}^{\infty} s(i)\eta_p(x-i), \tag{2.3}$$

where $\eta_p(x)$ is the cardinal spline of order p. In the frequency domain, cardinal splines converge to an ideal lowpass filter with cutoff frequency π (i.e., $\eta_p(x) \to \text{sinc}(x)$) as p tends to infinity [1, 45], which establishes the asymptotic equivalence with Shannon's sampling theorem [37].

Using (2.1) and (2.2) with (2.3) cardinal splines can be related to B-splines:

$$\eta_p(x) = \sum_{i=-\infty}^{\infty} b_p^{-1}(i)\beta_p(x-i). \tag{2.4}$$

Cardinal splines $\eta_p(x)$ and $\hat{\eta}_p(\omega)$ for $p \in \{0, 1, 2, 3, 4\}$ are shown in Figure 2.2.

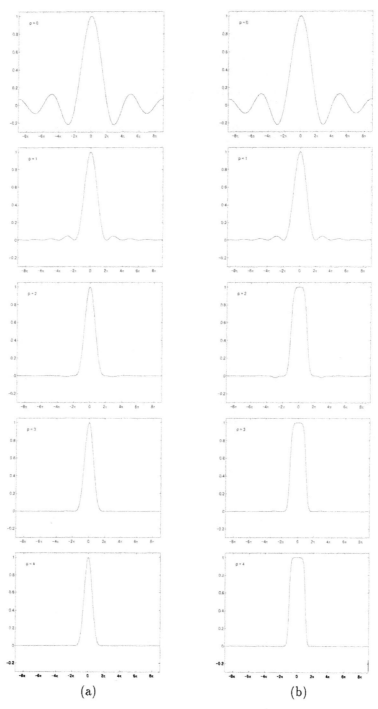

Figure 2.2: Fourier transforms of spline functions (a) $\hat{\beta}_p(\omega)$ and (b) $\hat{\eta}_p(\omega)$ for $p \in \{0, 1, 2, 3, 4\}$.

2.3 B-Spline Signal Approximations

Central B-splines are also simple to use when the goal is function approxima-tion. Least-squares B-spline approximation of $s(x) \in L^2(\boldsymbol{R})$ is achieved by computing the orthogonal projection of this function onto $\boldsymbol{S}^p$. We have

$$\tilde{s}(x) = s_p(x) = \sum_{i=-\infty}^{\infty} d(i)\beta_p(x - i) \tag{2.5}$$

with

$$d(i) = \langle s(x), \overset{\circ}{\beta}_p(x - i) \rangle, \tag{2.6}$$

where

$$\overset{\circ}{\beta}_p(x) = \sum_{i=-\infty}^{\infty} b_{2p+1}^{-1}(i)\beta_p(x - i)$$

is the dual spline of order p [45]. Spline functions $\beta_p(x)$ and $\overset{\circ}{\beta}_p(x)$ satisfy the biorthog-onality condition

$$\langle \beta_p(x - m), \overset{\circ}{\beta}_p(x - n) \rangle = \delta(m - n), \quad m, n \in \boldsymbol{Z}.$$

(Note that, since both $\beta_p(x)$ and $\overset{\circ}{\beta}_p(x)$ form a basis of $\boldsymbol{S}^p$, they can be interchanged in (2.5) and (2.6).)

Figure 2.3 shows functions $\overset{\circ}{\beta}_p(x)$ and their Fourier transforms $\overset{\hat{\circ}}{\beta}_p(\omega)$ for $p \in \{0, 1, 2, 3, 4\}$.

An interesting alternative to the minimum L^2-norm (i.e., least-squares) ap-proximation of a signal is obtained by computing oblique instead of orthogonal pro-jection of the signal onto the spline function space. Unser and Aldroubi proposed an independent specification of the sampling and approximation spaces [42]: a linear op-erator maps coefficients of the input signal expansion over sampling space basis into the coefficients of the approximation space basis expansion from which the signal's projection onto the approximation space is recovered. Constraining the entire system to be linear, shift-invariant for integer translations, and consistent (i.e., the system acts as an identity operator for functions that belong to the approximation space), the obtained solution for the signal approximation is the projection of a signal onto the approximation space perpendicular to the sampling space [42]. Analogously to (2.5) and (2.6) this projection can be expressed as

$$s_r(x) = \sum_{i=-\infty}^{\infty} a(i)\beta_r(x-i) \tag{2.7}$$

with

$$a(i) = q_{12}^{-1} * \langle s(x), \beta_s(x-i) \rangle,$$

where q_{12}^{-1} is the convolution inverse of the cross-correlation sequence

$$q_{12}(i) = \langle \beta_s(x-i), \beta_r(x) \rangle = b_{s+r+1}(i).$$

When the sampling space S^s and the approximation space S^r are identical (i.e., $s = r$), an orthogonal projection given by (2.5) and (2.6) results. (Note that the described oblique projection is not restricted to spline function spaces—the only requirement is that both sampling space basis and approximation space basis are Riesz bases of the corresponding function spaces [42].)

Signal approximation (2.7) is particularly attractive in situations where the sampling space is given *a priori* (e.g., by the impulse response of the acquisition device [42]) or when such an approximation is close to the optimal least-squares solution but simpler to implement than the orthogonal projection (e.g., [47]).

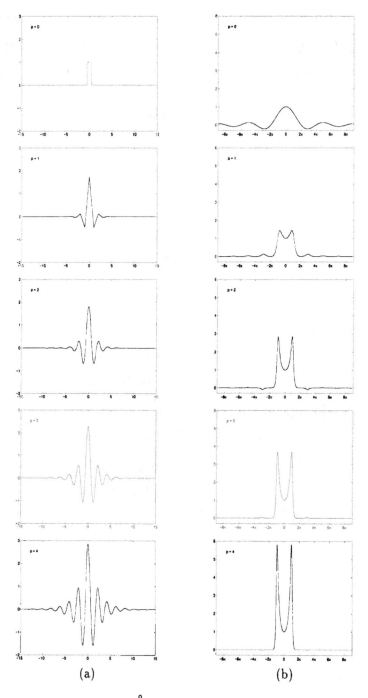

Figure 2.3: Spline functions (a) $\overset{\circ}{\beta}_p(x)$ and (b) their respective Fourier transforms $\overset{\circ}{\hat{\beta}}_p(\omega)$ for $p \in \{0, 1, 2, 3, 4\}$.

CHAPTER 3
TRANSFORM IN ONE DIMENSION

In this chapter, we will augment the one-dimensional discrete dyadic wavelet transform [28] to obtain a strong foundation for derivations of two-dimensional transforms in Chapter 4.

3.1 1-D Discrete Dyadic Wavelet Transform Revisited

A discrete wavelet transform is obtained from a continuous representation by discretizing dilation and translation parameters such that the resulting set of wavelets constitutes a frame. The dilation parameter is typically discretized by an exponential sampling with a fixed dilation step and the translation parameter by integer multiples of a fixed step [10]. Unfortunately, the resulting transform is variant under translations, a property which makes it less attractive for image analysis (cf. Section 1.1).

As we have already mentioned in Chapter 1, sampling the translation parameter with the same sampling period as the input function to the transform results in a translation-invariant, but redundant representation. The dyadic wavelet transform proposed by Mallat and Zhong [28] is one such representation. Let us begin with a brief review of properties of the dyadic wavelet transform as described in [28], but included here for completeness.

The dyadic wavelet transform of a function $s(x) \in L^2(\boldsymbol{R})$ is defined as a sequence of functions

$$\{W_m s(x)\}_{m \in \boldsymbol{Z}}, \tag{3.1}$$

17

where $W_m s(x) = s * \psi_m(x)$, and $\psi_m(x) = 2^{-m}\psi(2^{-m}x)$ is a wavelet $\psi(x)$ expanded by a dilation parameter (or scale) 2^m. Note the use of convolution instead of an inner product.

To ensure coverage of the frequency axis the requirement on the Fourier transform of $\psi_m(x)$ is the existence of $A_1 > 0$ and $B_1 < \infty$ such that

$$A_1 \leq \sum_{m=-\infty}^{\infty} |\hat{\psi}(2^m\omega)|^2 \leq B_1$$

is satisfied almost everywhere. The constraint on the Fourier transform of the (nonunique) reconstructing function $\chi(x)$ is

$$\sum_{m=-\infty}^{\infty} \hat{\psi}(2^m\omega)\,\hat{\chi}(2^m\omega) = 1.$$

A function $s(x)$ can then be completely reconstructed from its dyadic wavelet transform using the identity

$$s(x) = \sum_{m=-\infty}^{\infty} W_m s * \chi_m(x),$$

where $\chi_m(x) = 2^{-m}\chi(2^{-m}x)$.

In numerical applications, processing is performed on discrete rather than continuous functions. When the function to be transformed is in the discrete form, the scale 2^m can no longer vary over all $m \in Z$. Finite sampling rate prohibits the scale from being arbitrarily small, while computational resources restrict the use of an arbitrarily large scale. Let the finest scale be normalized to 1 and the coarsest scale set to 2^M.

The smoothing of a function $s(x) \in L^2(\boldsymbol{R})$ is defined as

$$S_m s(x) = s * \phi_m(x),$$

where $\phi_m(x) = 2^{-m}\phi(2^{-m}x)$ with $m \in Z$, and $\phi(x)$ is a smoothing function (i.e., its integral is equal to 1 and $\phi(x) \to 0$ as $|x| \to \infty$).

In [28], a real smoothing function $\phi(x)$ was selected, whose Fourier transform satisfied

$$|\hat{\phi}(\omega)|^2 = \sum_{m=1}^{\infty} \hat{\psi}(2^m \omega)\,\hat{\chi}(2^m \omega). \qquad (3.2)$$

In addition, it was shown that any discrete function of finite energy $s(n) \in l^2(\boldsymbol{Z})$ can be written as the uniform sampling of some function smoothed at scale 1, i.e., $s(n) = S_0 f(n)$, where $f(x) \in L^2(\boldsymbol{R})$ is not unique. Thus, the discrete dyadic wavelet transform of $s(n)$ for any coarse scale 2^M was defined as a sequence of discrete functions

$$\{S_M f(n+s), \{W_m f(n+s)\}_{m \in [1,M]}\}_{n \in \boldsymbol{Z}},$$

where s is a $\psi(x)$ dependent sampling shift.

The above initialization $s(n) = S_0 f(n)$ is rather standard in the discrete wavelet transform computation [10], although it yields correct results (i.e., the discrete wavelet transform is equal to the samples of its continuous counterpart) only when $s(n) = S_0 s(n)$. Here, we will concentrate on wavelets which are derivatives of spline functions and this will lead us to a simple initialization procedure [46] that alleviates the above problem.

For a certain choice of wavelets the discrete dyadic wavelet transform can be implemented within a fast hierarchical digital filtering scheme. Next, we shall summarize the relations between filters, wavelets, and smoothing functions.

First, let us introduce a real smoothing function $\varphi(x)$ such that (3.2) can be rewritten as[1]

$$\hat{\phi}(\omega)\,\hat{\varphi}(\omega) = \sum_{m=0}^{\infty} \hat{\psi}(2^m \omega)\,\hat{\chi}(2^m \omega), \qquad (3.3)$$

and let us set $\phi(x) = \beta_p(x)$ (i.e., we restrict ourselves to wavelets which are spline functions).

---

[1]Note that the sum index determines the range of scales of the discrete transform: using (3.2) we have $\hat{\psi}(2\omega)$ and $\hat{\chi}(2\omega)$ at the finest scale of the transform, while for (3.3) we get $\hat{\psi}(\omega)$ and $\hat{\chi}(\omega)$.

Computing (3.3) for the finest two scales shows that

$$\hat{\psi}(\omega)\,\hat{\chi}(\omega) = \hat{\beta}_p(\omega)\,\hat{\varphi}(\omega) - \hat{\beta}_p(2\omega)\,\hat{\varphi}(2\omega). \tag{3.4}$$

$\hat{\beta}_p(2\omega)$ can be related to $\hat{\beta}_p(\omega)$ by expressing $\hat{\beta}_p(2\omega)$ as (cf. Proposition 1 of [46])

$$\hat{\beta}_p(2\omega) = \frac{1}{2^{p+1}} \left(\frac{\sin(\omega)}{\sin\left(\frac{\omega}{2}\right)} \right)^{p+1} \left(\frac{\sin\left(\frac{\omega}{2}\right)}{\frac{\omega}{2}} \right)^{p+1},$$

and using $\sum_{m=0}^{M} e^{j(m\omega+\theta)} = \frac{\sin\left(\frac{(M+1)\omega}{2}\right)}{\sin\left(\frac{\omega}{2}\right)} e^{j\left(\frac{M\omega}{2}+\theta\right)}$:

$$\hat{\beta}_p(2\omega) = \left(\cos\left(\frac{\omega}{2}\right) \right)^{p+1} \hat{\beta}_p(\omega). \tag{3.5}$$

(Note that a relation similar to (3.5) can be derived for integer scales provided that the dilation parameter and the order p are not both even [46].)

Let $F(\omega)$ be a digital filter frequency response and let $F_s(\omega) = e^{j\omega s} F(\omega)$.

If we choose

$$\hat{\psi}(\omega) = G_{-s}(\omega)\,\hat{\beta}_p(\omega), \tag{3.6}$$

$$\hat{\varphi}(2\omega) = L_s(\omega)\,\hat{\varphi}(\omega), \tag{3.7}$$

$$\hat{\chi}(\omega) = K_s(\omega)\,\hat{\varphi}(\omega), \tag{3.8}$$

and

$$H(\omega) = e^{j\omega s} \left(\cos\left(\frac{\omega}{2}\right) \right)^{p+1}, \tag{3.9}$$

where $s \in \{0, \frac{1}{2}\}$ is a filter dependent sampling shift needed for $g(n)$, $l(n)$, $k(n)$, and $h(n)$ to be FIR filters, and insert Equations (3.5)–(3.9) into (3.4), we observe the relation between frequency responses of the filters

$$G(\omega)K(\omega) + H(\omega)L(\omega) = 1. \tag{3.10}$$

Similar to orthogonal and biorthogonal discrete wavelet transforms, the discrete dyadic wavelet transform can be implemented within a hierarchical filtering scheme. To derive such a digital filtering scheme, let us assume that $\hat{s}(\omega)$ from (3.1) is bandlimited to $[-\pi, \pi]$. Using Shannon's sampling theorem [37] and (3.6) in the definition of the dyadic wavelet transform (3.1) with $m=0$ shows

$$W_0 s(x) = \int_{-\infty}^{\infty} \sum_{i=-\infty}^{\infty} s(i) \text{sinc}(t-i) \sum_{m=-\infty}^{\infty} g_{-s}(m) \beta_p(x-t-m) \, dt.$$

By making use of the fact that the cardinal spline functions tend to the sinc function as their order r approaches infinity, and employing (2.4) we can write

$$\widehat{W_0 s}(\omega) \simeq S(\omega) B_r^{-1}(\omega) \hat{\beta}_r(\omega) \, \hat{\beta}_p(\omega) \, G_{-s}(\omega),$$

or, by using (3.5) and (3.9),

$$\mathcal{F}\{ W_m s(x)|_{x=n} \} \simeq S(\omega) \, B_r^{-1}(\omega) \, B_{p+r+1}(\omega) \, G_{-s}(2^m \omega) \prod_{i=0}^{m-1} H_{-s}(2^i \omega). \qquad (3.11)$$

Equation (3.11) entirely specifies the discrete dyadic wavelet transform decomposition, while the reconstruction follows from (3.4)–(3.9). Three levels of a filter bank implementation are shown in Figure 3.1. (Note that the initialization is the same as the one proposed in [46] and that except for the prefiltering and postfiltering, this scheme is implementing "algorithme à trous.") Noninteger shifts at scale 1 for filters with $s = \frac{1}{2}$ are rounded to the nearest integer.

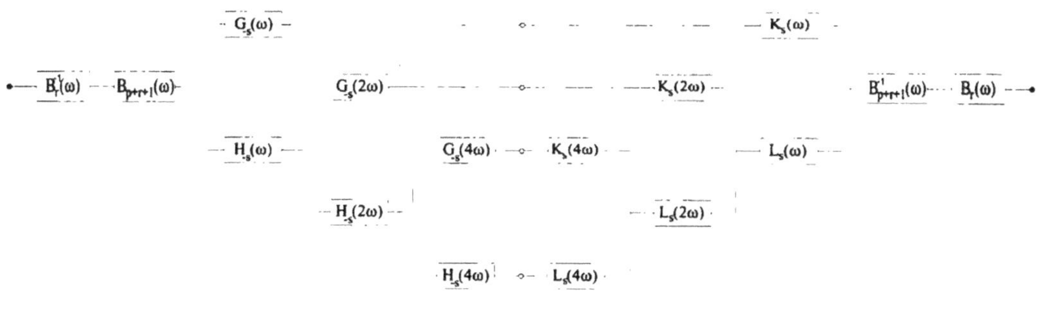

Figure 3.1: Filter bank implementation of a one-dimensional discrete dyadic wavelet transform decomposition (left) and reconstruction (right) for three levels of analysis.

We will now perform a simple experiment which will illustrate the difference between the implementation of the discrete dyadic wavelet transform as originally proposed in [28] (i.e., without prefiltering and postfiltering) and the one from Figure 3.1.

Let $s(x) = \text{sinc}(x)$, $p = 2$, and $g(n) = 2\delta(n+1) - 2\delta(n)$ (this particular choice for p and $g(n)$ results in the same wavelet as was used by Mallat and collaborators [27, 28]). The dyadic wavelet transform of $s(x)$ at a scale 2^m (3.1) in the frequency domain is then

$$\widehat{W_m s}(\omega) = G_{-s}(2^m\omega)\,\hat{\beta}_2(2^m\omega)\,\text{rect}\left(\frac{\omega}{2\pi}\right). \tag{3.12}$$

The Fourier transform of the discrete dyadic wavelet transform of $s(n) = \delta(n)$ at a scale 2^m using spline based initialization follows from (3.11)

$$\mathcal{F}\{\widetilde{W}_m s(n)\} = B_r^{-1}(\omega)\,B_{r+3}(\omega)\,G_{-s}(2^m\omega)\prod_{i=0}^{m-1} H_{-s}(2^i\omega), \tag{3.13}$$

while the one using the algorithm from [28] equals

$$\mathcal{F}\{\widetilde{W}_m s(n)\} = G_{-s}(2^m\omega)\prod_{i=0}^{m-1} H_{-s}(2^i\omega). \tag{3.14}$$

In Figure 3.2 a comparison of magnitudes of (3.13) and (3.14) versus (3.12) is shown: in Figure 3.2(a) magnitudes of (3.12) (solid) and (3.14) (dashed) are plotted for $m \in \{0, 1, 2, 3\}$, while the dashed curves in 3.2(b) represent magnitudes of (3.13) with $r = 5$.

By choosing the appropriate order r, (3.13) can approximate (3.12) in the interval $[-\pi, \pi]$ arbitrarily good, while originally proposed (3.14) has troubles at finer scales. Mallat and Zhong [28] noticed that there was a problem with their discrete transform computation, and introduced a set of constants associated with the discrete transform coefficients at dyadic scales. They chose the values of constants such that the transform coefficient modulus maxima remained constant over all dyadic scales for a step edge input signal. In relation to Figure 3.2(a) this is equivalent to multiplying $\mathcal{F}\{\widetilde{W}_m s(n)\}$ by a distinct constant for each m. Clearly, this can improve over the situation depicted by Figure 3.2(a), but can still not compete with the described spline based initialization.

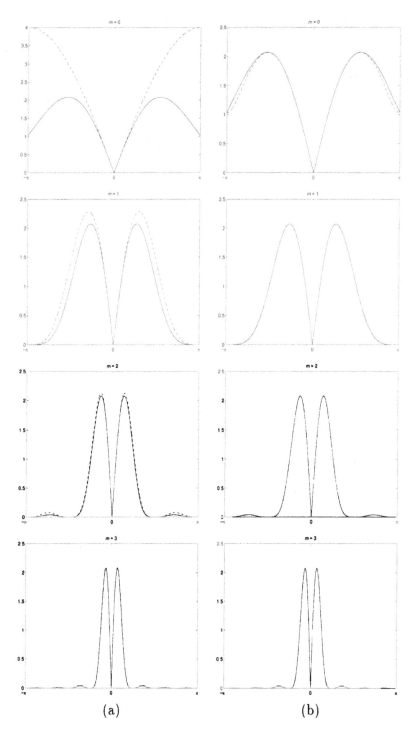

Figure 3.2: (a) Fourier transform magnitudes of the dyadic wavelet transform of $s(x) = \text{sinc}(x)$ (solid) and the originally proposed discrete dyadic wavelet transform [28] of $s(n) = \delta(n)$ (dashed). (b) Fourier transform magnitudes of the dyadic wavelet transform of $s(x)$ (solid) and the discrete dyadic wavelet transform using quintic splines for interpolation of $s(n)$ (dashed).

Next, we will choose filters in the filter bank implementation of the discrete dyadic wavelet transform. As already mentioned, we are interested in wavelets which are derivatives of spline functions. $G(\omega)$ in (3.6) is therefore the Fourier transform of the difference operator centered around $-s$ (cf. Property 4 in Section 2):

$$G(\omega) = e^{j\omega s} \left(2j \sin\left(\frac{\omega}{2}\right) \right)^d, \qquad (3.15)$$

where d is the order of the derivative and the sampling shift for this filter is $s = \frac{d \bmod 2}{2}$.

Since $H(\omega)$ was already given by (3.9), the remaining two filters to be determined are $L(\omega)$ and $K(\omega)$. Both of them are (as is true for $\varphi(x)$ and $\chi(x)$) nonunique.

If we choose $L(\omega)$ such that we can express $K(\omega)$ in terms of a finite geometric series having the smallest number of elements for an arbitrary p, we get

$$L(\omega) = e^{-j\omega s} \sum_{m=1}^{\lfloor \frac{d+1}{2} \rfloor} (-1)^{m+1} \binom{\lfloor \frac{d+1}{2} \rfloor}{m} \left(\cos\left(\frac{\omega}{2}\right) \right)^{(p+1)(2m-1)} \qquad (3.16)$$

and

$$K(\omega) = \frac{1}{(2j)^d} \left(e^{-j\omega s} \sin\left(\frac{\omega}{2}\right) \right)^{d \bmod 2} \left(\sum_{m=0}^{p} \left(\cos\left(\frac{\omega}{2}\right) \right)^{2m} \right)^{\lfloor \frac{d+1}{2} \rfloor}, \qquad (3.17)$$

where $\lfloor x \rfloor$ denotes the largest integer smaller than x, the sampling shift for $L(\omega)$ is the same as the one for $H(\omega)$ (i.e., $s = \frac{(p+1) \bmod 2}{2}$), and the sampling shift for $K(\omega)$ is the same as the one for $G(\omega)$.

Note that Equations (3.9) and (3.15)–(3.17) work fine from the mathematical point of view, but in practice the reconstruction may become cumbersome when both p and d are large (the lengths of impulse responses $h(n)$, $g(n)$, $l(n)$, and $k(n)$ are $p+2$, $d+1$, $(p+1)(d-(d+1) \bmod 2)+1$, and $pd+(p+1)(d \bmod 2)+1$, respectively, while for the frequency responses of the decomposition filters we observe that $\lim_{p \to \infty} |H_{-s}(\omega)| = \delta_u(\omega + 2n\pi)$ and $\lim_{d \to \infty} (2j)^{-d} |G_{-s}(\omega)| = \delta_u(\omega + (2n+1)\pi)$ with $n \in \mathbf{Z}$).

It is also worth noting that $K(\omega)$ is a lowpass filter when p is even (i.e., the reconstruction function $\chi(x)$ is a wavelet only for p odd).

Tables 3.1, 3.2, and 3.3 list impulse responses of the four filters for $p \in \{0, 1, 2\}$ and $d \in \{1, 2, 3\}$, while Figure 3.3 shows wavelets $\psi(x) = \frac{d^d \beta_{p+d}(x)}{dx^d}$ for the same values of p and d. Wavelets from this family have a support of length $d+p+1$, regularity order p, and are either symmetric or antisymmetric.

Table 3.1: Impulse responses $h(n)$, $g(n)$, $l(n)$, and $k(n)$ for $p=0$ and $d \in \{1, 2, 3\}$.

n	$h(n)$	$d=1$			$d=2$			$d=3$		
		$g(n)$	$l(n)$	$k(n)$	$g(n)$	$l(n)$	$k(n)$	$g(n)$	$l(n)$	$k(n)$
-2								1		
-1	0.5	1			1			-3	-0.125	
0	0.5	-1	0.5	-0.25	-2	0.5	-0.25	3	0.625	0.0625
1			0.5	0.25	1	0.5		-1	0.625	-0.0625
2									-0.125	

Table 3.2: Impulse responses $h(n)$, $g(n)$, $l(n)$, and $k(n)$ for $p=1$ and $d \in \{1, 2, 3\}$.

n	$h(n)$ / $l(n)$	$d=1$		$d=2$	
		$g(n)$	$k(n)$	$g(n)$	$k(n)$
-1	0.25	1	-0.0625	1	-0.0625
0	0.5	-1	-0.3125	-2	-0.375
1	0.25		0.3125	1	-0.0625
2			0.0625		

n	$h(n)$	$g(n)$	$d=3$ $l(n)$	$k(n)$
-3			-0.015625	
-2		1	-0.09375	0.00390625
-1	0.25	-3	0.265625	0.04296875
0	0.5	3	0.6875	0.1015625
1	0.25	-1	0.265625	-0.1015625
2			-0.09375	-0.04296875
3			-0.015625	-0.00390625

As already discussed, wavelets with $p=2$ and $d=1$ from a family of wavelets with p even and $d=1$ were used in [27, 28], whereas filters with $p=1$ and $d=2$ from a family of filters with p odd and $d=2$ were employed by Laine and collaborators [11, 22, 23]. Here described transform puts no restrictions on the choice of p or d whatsoever, and uses a better initialization procedure than the one originally proposed in [28].

Table 3.3: Impulse responses $h(n)$, $g(n)$, $l(n)$, and $k(n)$ for $p=2$ and $d \in \{1,2,3\}$.

		$d = 1$			$d = 2$		
n	$h(n)$	$g(n)$	$l(n)$	$k(n)$	$g(n)$	$l(n)$	$k(n)$
-2	0.125			-0.015625			-0.015625
-1	0.375	1	0.125	-0.109375	1	0.125	-0.125
0	0.375	-1	0.375	-0.34375	-2	0.375	-0.46875
1	0.125		0.375	0.34375	1	0.375	-0.125
2			0.125	0.109375		0.125	-0.015625
3				0.015625			

			$d = 3$	
n	$h(n)$	$g(n)$	$l(n)$	$k(n)$
-4			-0.001953125	0.000244140625
-3			-0.017578125	0.003662109375
-2	0.125	1	-0.0703125	0.0263671875
-1	0.375	-3	0.085937	0.0908203125
0	0.375	3	0.50390625	0.13037109375
1	0.125	-1	0.50390625	-0.13037109375
2			0.0859375	-0.0908203125
3			-0.0703125	-0.0263671875
4			-0.017578125	-0.003662109375
5			-0.001953125	-0.000244140625

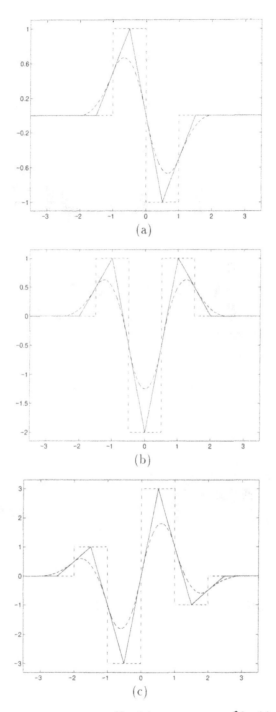

Figure 3.3: (a) Wavelets (a) $\psi(x) = \frac{d\beta_{p+1}(x)}{dx}$, (b) $\psi(x) = \frac{d^2\beta_{p+2}(x)}{dx^2}$, and (c) $\psi(x) = \frac{d^3\beta_{p+3}(x)}{dx^3}$ for $p=0$ (dashdotted), $p=1$ (solid), and $p=2$ (dashed).

Page
Missing
or
Unavailable

the zero-crossings of $W_m s(x)$ for $d = 2$, a scale-space image of the representation similar to [48] can be obtained. The only differences are that curves in the scale-space plane are computed for dyadic scales only and that ϑ_m is a close approximation of a Gaussian instead of a true Gaussian.

CHAPTER 4
TRANSFORMS IN TWO DIMENSIONS

In this chapter, we will extend the one-dimensional transform from Chapter 3 to two dimensions[1] and derive several two-dimensional transforms with translation and at least approximately rotation-invariant decomposition.

4.1 2-D Discrete Dyadic Wavelet Transform Revisited

The dyadic wavelet transform of a function $s(x, y) \in L^2(\mathbf{R}^2)$ is defined as a set of functions [28]

$$\{W_m^1 s(x, y), W_m^2 s(x, y)\}_{m \in \mathbf{Z}}, \tag{4.1}$$

where $W_m^i s(x, y) = s * \psi_m^i(x, y)$ for $i = \{1, 2\}$ and $\psi_m^i(x, y) = 2^{-2m} \psi^i(2^{-m} x, 2^{-m} y)$ are wavelets $\psi^i(x, y)$ expanded by a dilation parameter 2^m.

To ensure coverage of the frequency space there must exist an $A_2 > 0$ and $B_2 < \infty$ such that

$$A_2 \leq \sum_{m=-\infty}^{\infty} \sum_{i=1}^{2} |\hat{\psi}^i(2^m \omega_x, 2^m \omega_y)|^2 \leq B_2$$

is satisfied almost everywhere. If (nonunique) functions $\chi^1(x, y)$, $\chi^2(x, y)$ are chosen such that their Fourier transforms satisfy

$$\sum_{m=-\infty}^{\infty} \sum_{i=1}^{2} \hat{\psi}^i(2^m \omega_x, 2^m \omega_y) \, \hat{\chi}^i(2^m \omega_x, 2^m \omega_y) = 1,$$

the function $s(x, y)$ may be reconstructed from its dyadic wavelet transform by

$$s(x, y) = \sum_{m=-\infty}^{\infty} \sum_{i=1}^{2} W_m^i s * \chi_m^i(x, y),$$

where $\chi_m^i(x, y) = 2^{-2m} \chi^i(2^{-m} x, 2^{-m} y)$.

---

[1] For extensions to higher dimensions, please refer to [18, 19].

However, when processing discrete functions the scale 2^m may no longer vary over all $m \in \mathbf{Z}$. Let the finest scale be normalized to 1 and the coarsest scale set to be 2^M. Let us, similar to [28], introduce a real smoothing function $\phi(x,y)$ such that its Fourier transform satisfies

$$|\hat{\phi}(\omega_x, \omega_y)|^2 = \sum_{m=0}^{\infty} \sum_{i=1}^{2} \hat{\psi}^i(2^m\omega_x, 2^m\omega_y)\hat{\chi}^i(2^m\omega_x, 2^m\omega_y). \qquad (4.2)$$

Here, as in one dimension, a finite energy discrete function $(s(n_x, n_y) \in l^2(\mathbf{Z}^2))$ can be written as the uniform sampling of some function smoothed at scale 1: $s(n_x, n_y) = S_0 f(n_x, n_y)$, where $f(x,y) \in L^2(\mathbf{R}^2)$ is not unique, and $S_m f(x,y) = f * \phi_m(x,y)$. This led Mallat and Zhong [28] to a two-dimensional analog of the one-dimensional definition of the discrete dyadic wavelet transform:[2]

$$\{S_{M-1}f(n_x+s, n_y+s), \{W_m^1 f(n_x+s, n_y+s), W_m^2 f(n_x+s, n_y+s)\}_{m\in[0,M-1]}\}_{(n_x,n_y)\in\mathbf{Z}^2}.$$

We will use, as in Section 3.1, a spline-based initialization procedure.

To implement a multidimensional discrete dyadic wavelet transform within a fast hierarchical digital filtering scheme, the wavelets were chosen to be separable products of one-dimensional functions:

$$\psi^1(x,y) = \psi(x)\,\phi(y), \qquad (4.3)$$

$$\psi^2(x,y) = \psi(y)\,\phi(x), \qquad (4.4)$$

where $\phi(x)$ and $\psi(x)$ were chosen as described in Section 3.1 (i.e., $\phi(x) = \beta_p(x)$ and $\hat{\psi}(\omega)$ specified by (3.6)).

From (4.3), (4.4), and (3.6), we may write

$$\hat{\psi}^1(\omega_x, \omega_y) = G_{-s}(\omega_x)\,\hat{\beta}_p(\omega_x)\hat{\beta}_p(\omega_y), \qquad (4.5)$$

$$\hat{\psi}^2(\omega_x, \omega_y) = G_{-s}(\omega_y)\,\hat{\beta}_p(\omega_x)\hat{\beta}_p(\omega_y), \qquad (4.6)$$

---

[2]As in Section 3.1, we put the finest scale of the transform at $m = 0$.

where $G(\omega)$ is given by (3.15) for $d \in \{1, 2\}$. Choosing

$$\hat{\chi}^1(\omega_x, \omega_y) = K_s(\omega_x) T_1(\omega_y) \hat{\beta}_p(\omega_x) \hat{\beta}_p(\omega_y), \tag{4.7}$$

$$\hat{\chi}^2(\omega_x, \omega_y) = K_s(\omega_y) T_1(\omega_x) \hat{\beta}_p(\omega_x) \hat{\beta}_p(\omega_y), \tag{4.8}$$

where $K(\omega)$ and $T_1(\omega)$ are digital filter frequency responses, we may compute (4.2) for the finest two scales by

$$\sum_{i=1}^2 \hat{\psi}^i(2\omega_x, 2\omega_y)\, \hat{\chi}^i(2\omega_x, 2\omega_y) = |\hat{\phi}(\omega_x, \omega_y)|^2 - |\hat{\phi}(2\omega_x, 2\omega_y)|^2. \tag{4.9}$$

Inserting the terms defined by (4.5), (4.6), (4.7), (4.8), (3.5), and (3.9) with $\hat{\phi}(\omega_x, \omega_y) = \hat{\beta}_p(\omega_x)\hat{\beta}_p(\omega_y)$ into (4.9) results in

$$K(\omega_x)G(\omega_x)T_1(\omega_y) + K(\omega_y)G(\omega_y)T_1(\omega_x) + |H(\omega_x)|^2|H(\omega_y)|^2 = 1. \tag{4.10}$$

Equation (4.10) represents a relation between the frequency responses of the digital filters used to implement a multidimensional discrete dyadic wavelet transform and is a multidimensional analog to (3.10).

Solving (4.10) for $T_1(\omega)$ by substituting $K(\omega)G(\omega)$ from (3.10) yields the closed formula [28]

$$T_1(\omega) = \frac{1}{2}\left(1 + |H(\omega)|^2\right) \tag{4.11}$$

In Table 4.1 we provide the filter coefficients for $T_1(\omega)$ from (4.11) for $p \in \{0, 1, 2\}$. All other filters from (4.10) were already specified in Section 3.1.

Table 4.1: Impulse responses $t_1(n)$ for $p \in \{0, 1, 2\}$.

n	p=0	p=1	p=2
-3			0.0078125
-2		0.03125	0.046875
-1	0.125	0.125	0.1171875
0	0.75	0.6875	0.65625
1	0.125	0.125	0.1171875
2		0.03125	0.046875
3			0.0078125

As in the one-dimensional case, a two-dimensional discrete dyadic wavelet transform can be implemented as a fast hierarchical filtering scheme. To derive such an implementation, we, similar to the one-dimensional case from Section 3.1, use the definition of the two-dimensional dyadic wavelet transform (4.1) and require $\hat{s}(\omega_x, \omega_y) = 0$ for $|\omega_x| > \pi$ or $|\omega_y| > \pi$. Using Shannon's sampling theorem in two dimensions [16], (4.5), (4.6), and $m = 0$, we get

$$W_0^1 s(x,y) = \int_{-\infty}^{\infty} \int_{-\infty}^{\infty} \sum_{i_x=-\infty}^{\infty} \sum_{i_y=-\infty}^{\infty} s(i_x, i_y) \operatorname{sinc}(t_x - i_x) \operatorname{sinc}(t_y - i_y) \cdot$$
$$\cdot \sum_{m=-\infty}^{\infty} g_{-s}(m) \beta_p(x - t_x - m) \beta_p(y - t_y)\, dt_x\, dt_y$$

and

$$W_0^2 s(x,y) = \int_{-\infty}^{\infty} \int_{-\infty}^{\infty} \sum_{i_x=-\infty}^{\infty} \sum_{i_y=-\infty}^{\infty} s(i_x, i_y) \operatorname{sinc}(t_x - i_x) \operatorname{sinc}(t_y - i_y) \cdot$$
$$\cdot \beta_p(x - t_x) \sum_{m=-\infty}^{\infty} g_{-s}(m) \beta_p(y - t_y - m)\, dt_x\, dt_y.$$

As in one dimension, we make use of the fact that the cardinal spline functions converge to the sinc function as their order r tends to infinity, and write

$$\widehat{W_0^1 s}(\omega_x, \omega_y) \simeq S(\omega_x, \omega_y) B_r^{-1}(\omega_x) B_r^{-1}(\omega_y) \hat{\beta}_{p+r+1}(\omega_x) \hat{\beta}_{p+r+1}(\omega_y)\, G_{-s}(\omega_x)$$

and

$$\widehat{W_0^2 s}(\omega_x, \omega_y) \simeq S(\omega_x, \omega_y) B_r^{-1}(\omega_x) B_r^{-1}(\omega_y) \hat{\beta}_{p+r+1}(\omega_x) \hat{\beta}_{p+r+1}(\omega_y)\, G_{-s}(\omega_y),$$

or for $m \in [0, M)$ and discrete signal processing

$$\mathcal{F}\{W_m^1 s(x,y)\big|_{x=n_x, y=n_y}\} \simeq S(\omega_x, \omega_y)\, B_r^{-1}(\omega_x)\, B_r^{-1}(\omega_y)\, B_{p+r+1}(\omega_x) \cdot$$
$$\cdot B_{p+r+1}(\omega_y)\, G_{-s}(2^m \omega_x) \prod_{i=0}^{m-1} H_{-s}(2^i \omega_x) H_{-s}(2^i \omega_y). \qquad (4.12)$$

and

$$\mathcal{F}\{W_m^2 s(x,y)\big|_{x=n_x, y=n_y}\} \simeq S(\omega_x, \omega_y)\, B_r^{-1}(\omega_x)\, B_r^{-1}(\omega_y)\, B_{p+r+1}(\omega_x) \cdot$$
$$\cdot B_{p+r+1}(\omega_y)\, G_{-s}(2^m \omega_y) \prod_{i=0}^{m-1} H_{-s}(2^i \omega_x) H_{-s}(2^i \omega_y). \qquad (4.13)$$

Equations (4.12) and (4.13) describe the decomposition part of the filter bank implementation of a two-dimensional discrete dyadic wavelet transform. The reconstruction part can be obtained from (4.7)–(4.9) with (3.5) and (3.9). The entire filter bank implementation of the transform is shown in Figure 4.1. Except for the prefiltering and postfiltering, we readily recognize the implementation proposed in [28].

Using the fact that a wavelet $\psi(x)$ is equal to a first $(d=1)$ or a second $(d=2)$ derivative of a spline function $\beta_{p+d}(x)$, (4.3) and (4.4) may be rewritten as

$$\psi^i(x,y) = \frac{\partial^d \vartheta^i(x,y)}{\partial x_i^d}, \quad i,d \in \{1,2\},$$

where

$$\vartheta^1(x,y) = \beta_{p+d}(x)\,\beta_p(y)$$

and

$$\vartheta^2(x,y) = \beta_p(x)\,\beta_{p+d}(y).$$

Let us denote $\vec{W}_m s(x,y) = (W_m^1 s(x,y), W_m^2 s(x,y))$, $\vec{\nabla} = (\frac{\partial}{\partial x}, \frac{\partial}{\partial y})$, $\Delta = \vec{\nabla}^2 = (\frac{\partial^2}{\partial x^2} + \frac{\partial^2}{\partial y^2})$, and assume that $\vartheta^i(x,y,)$ can be approximated by $\vartheta(x,y)$ for both $i \in \{1,2\}$.

For $d=1$ it then follows that

$$\vec{W}_m s(x,y) = 2^m \vec{\nabla}(s * \vartheta_m)(x,y). \qquad (4.14)$$

Thus for $d=2$ we can write

$$\sum_{i=1}^{2} W_m^i s(x,y) = 2^{2m} \Delta(s * \vartheta_m)(x,y). \qquad (4.15)$$

With $\vartheta(x,y)$ being a Gaussian, finding local extrema of (4.14) in the direction of gradient $\vec{\nabla}$ corresponds to the filtering stage of a Canny edge detector [6], and finding zero-crossings of (4.15) corresponds to the filtering carried out with a Marr-Hildreth edge detector (Laplacian of Gaussian) [29]. (Note that both edge detectors

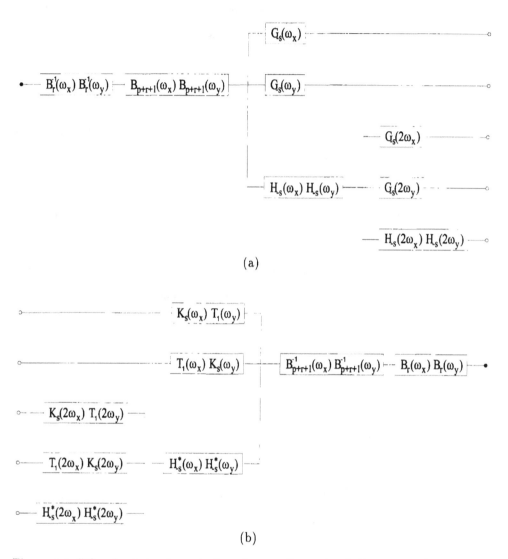

(a)

(b)

Figure 4.1: Filter bank implementation of a two-dimensional discrete dyadic wavelet transform (a) decomposition and (b) reconstruction for two levels of analysis. $H^*_{-s}(\omega)$ denotes the complex conjugate of $H_{-s}(\omega)$.

involve postprocessing). Edge detection based on finding local extrema of $\vec{W}_m s(x,y)$ or zero-crossings of $\sum_{i=1}^{2} W_m^i s(x,y)$ is therefore an approximation to the Canny or the Marr-Hildreth edge detector over a range of dyadic scales. The differences stem from the fact that $\vartheta(x,y)$ is neither a Gaussian nor is $\vartheta^i(x,y)$ equal to $\vartheta(x,y)$.

4.2 Steerable Functions

When extending the transform from Chapter 3 to two dimensions, one of the first questions that come to mind is how to deal with the fact that derivatives can be defined in any direction of the plane.[3] In case of a first derivative of a Gaussian, one can simply compute first derivatives of a Gaussian in x and y directions and then determine the derivative in any direction from these two directional derivatives [6]. For higher order derivatives of a Gaussian, Freeman and Adelson [12] showed that order+1 directional operators are needed for synthesizing the operator at any orientation. In fact, functions with the property of expressing their arbitrary rotations as linear combinations of some functions are not limited to derivatives of a Gaussian. Below, we briefly restate some of the results from [12].

A two-dimensional function is called "steerable" if its rotations generate a finite dimensional space. Rotations of a steerable function $f(r,\theta)$ can therefore be expressed as

$$f(r, \theta - \theta_0) = \sum_{i=1}^{I} c_i(\theta_0)\, f_i(r,\theta), \tag{4.16}$$

where θ_0 denotes an arbitrary angle, $\{c_i(\theta_0)\}$ stands for a set of interpolating functions, $\{f_i(r,\theta)\}$ is a set of basis functions, and $r = \sqrt{x^2+y^2}$ and $\theta = \arg(x,y)$ are polar radius and angle, respectively.

If $f(r,\theta)$ represents a filter kernel, the result of filtering with a rotated filter $f(r, \theta - \theta_0)$ can be computed simply by $\{c_i(\theta_0)\}$ weighted linear combination of outputs from basis filters $\{f_i(r,\theta)\}$. Only the outputs from basis filters need to be

---

[3]Second derivatives of central B-splines can be used, as we saw in Section 4.1, to approximate Laplacian of a Gaussian for approximately rotation-invariant, although not directional, processing.

precomputed and then the output from a filter rotated by any angle θ_0 can be found by interpolating between them. When a large number of rotations of a template filter is required, the above scheme can lead to substantial savings in both computational cost (time) and memory requirements (space).

The necessary condition for a function $f(r, \theta)$ to be steerable is that $f(r, \theta)$ is bandlimited in its polar angle:

$$f(r, \theta) = \sum_{n=-N}^{N} a_n(r) e^{jn\theta}. \qquad (4.17)$$

This can be verified by inserting (4.17) into (4.16) and by assuming, for convenience, that $f_i(r, \theta) = f(r, \theta - \theta_i)$:

$$a_n(r) e^{-jn\theta_0} = \sum_{i=1}^{I} c_i(\theta_0) a_n(r) e^{-jn\theta_i}, \qquad (4.18)$$

where $\{\theta_i\}$ is a set of user defined angles and $n \in [-N, 0]$. [4] Since only nonzero coefficients $a_n(r)$ are of interest, both sides of (4.18) can be divided by $a_n(r)$. This yields a matrix equation from which interpolating functions $c_i(\theta_0)$ can be determined:

$$\begin{bmatrix} 1 \\ e^{j\theta_0} \\ \vdots \\ e^{jN\theta_0} \end{bmatrix} = \begin{bmatrix} 1 & 1 & \cdots & 1 \\ e^{j\theta_1} & e^{j\theta_2} & \cdots & e^{j\theta_I} \\ \vdots & \vdots & & \vdots \\ e^{jN\theta_1} & e^{jN\theta_2} & \cdots & e^{jN\theta_I} \end{bmatrix} \begin{bmatrix} c_1(\theta_0) \\ c_2(\theta_0) \\ \vdots \\ c_I(\theta_0) \end{bmatrix}. \qquad (4.19)$$

For coefficients $a_n = 0$ the rows corresponding to each n were removed from the matrix formulation shown in (4.19). For this system to have a solution, the angles $\{\theta_i\}$ must be chosen such that the columns of the matrix are linearly independent.

In [12] they proved that the minimum number of basis functions $f_i(r, \theta)$ needed to steer $f(r, \theta)$ according to (4.16) is equal to the number of nonzero coefficients $a_n(r)$ in the Fourier series expansion (4.17).

To conclude this brief description of steerability, let us only remark that functions which are not steerable (i.e., do not have a finite number of terms in (4.17))

---

[4]Note that the constraints are the same for $n \in [-N, -1]$ and $n \in [1, N]$, so that a subset of all possible values for $n \in [-N, N]$ can be taken.

can be approximated with steerable functions (a singular value decomposition was employed for approximating such functions efficiently [31]), and that the technique of expressing transformed versions of a function as linear combinations of a fixed set of basis functions is not limited to rotations (extensions to translations [39], scalings [31, 39], and general transformations [14] have been reported).

4.3   Steerable Dyadic Wavelet Transform

Returning to the question from the beginning of Section 4.2, the answer seems obvious: one needs to construct a steerable analog to the one-dimensional transform from Chapter 3. Steerable transforms are nothing new—quite a few [13, 17, 38, 39] have been devised, some of them [17, 38] exactly for the computation of directional derivatives. Here, we are not interested in any directional derivatives: we want to use derivatives of central B-splines which, as the order of B-splines increases, tend to derivatives of a Gaussian.

We define a steerable dyadic wavelet transform of a function $s(x, y) \in L^2(\mathbf{R}^2)$ at a scale 2^m, $m \in \mathbf{Z}$, as [21]

$$W_m^i s(x, y) = s * \psi_m^i(x, y), \tag{4.20}$$

where $\psi_m^i(x, y)$ denotes $\psi_m(x, y)$ rotated by θ_i, $\psi_m(x, y) = 2^{-2m}\psi(2^{-m}x, 2^{-m}y)$, $\psi(x, y)$ is a steerable wavelet that can be steered with I basis functions, and $\theta_i = \frac{i-1}{I}\pi$ with $i \in \{1, 2, \dots, I\}$.

Analogously to the one-dimensional case (cf. Section 3.1) we require the two-dimensional Fourier plane to be covered by the dyadic dilations of $\hat{\psi}^i(2^m\omega_x, 2^m\omega_y)$: there must exist $A_3 > 0$ and $B_3 < \infty$ such that

$$A_3 \leq \sum_{m=-\infty}^{\infty} \sum_{i=1}^{I} |\hat{\psi}^i(2^m\omega_x, 2^m\omega_y)|^2 \leq B_3 \tag{4.21}$$

is satisfied almost everywhere.

If (nonunique) reconstructing functions $\chi_m^i(x,y)$ are chosen such that their Fourier transforms satisfy

$$\sum_{m=-\infty}^{\infty} \sum_{i=1}^{I} \hat{\psi}^i(2^m \omega_x, 2^m \omega_y) \, \hat{\chi}^i(2^m \omega_x, 2^m \omega_y) = 1, \qquad (4.22)$$

the function $s(x,y)$ may be reconstructed from its steerable dyadic wavelet transform by

$$s(x,y) = \sum_{m=-\infty}^{\infty} \sum_{i=1}^{I} W_m^i s * \chi_m^i(x,y), \qquad (4.23)$$

where $\chi_m^i(x,y)$ denotes $\chi_m(x,y)$ rotated by θ_i and $\chi_m(x,y) = 2^{-2m} \chi(2^{-m}x, 2^{-m}y)$.

To derive an algorithm for the fast computation of the transform, we, similar to (3.3), introduce two smoothing functions such that

$$\hat{\phi}(\omega_x, \omega_y) \, \hat{\varphi}(\omega_x, \omega_y) = \sum_{m=0}^{\infty} \sum_{i=1}^{I} \hat{\psi}^i(2^m \omega_x, 2^m \omega_y) \, \hat{\chi}^i(2^m \omega_x, 2^m \omega_y). \qquad (4.24)$$

We choose wavelets that are steerable analogs to the one-dimensional wavelets from Section 3.1:[5]

$$\hat{\psi}(\omega_r, \omega_\theta) = (j\omega_r \cos(\omega_\theta))^d \left(\frac{\sin(\frac{\omega_r}{2})}{\frac{\omega_r}{2}} \right)^{p+d+1}, \qquad (4.25)$$

where $\omega_r = \sqrt{\omega_x^2 + \omega_y^2}$ and $\omega_\theta = \arg(\omega_x, \omega_y)$. These wavelets can be steered with $d+1$ basis functions (i.e., I in (4.16) is equal to $d+1$).

Choosing

$$\hat{\phi}(2\omega_r) = H_{st}(\omega_r) \, \hat{\phi}(\omega_r), \qquad (4.26)$$

$$\hat{\psi}^i(\omega_r, \omega_\theta) = G_{st}(\omega_r, \omega_\theta - \theta_i) \, \hat{\phi}(\omega_r), \qquad (4.27)$$

$$\hat{\varphi}(2\omega_r) = L_{st}(\omega_r) \, \hat{\varphi}(\omega_r), \qquad (4.28)$$

and

$$\hat{\chi}^i(\omega_r, \omega_\theta) = K_{st}(\omega_r, \omega_\theta - \theta_i) \, \hat{\varphi}(\omega_r), \qquad (4.29)$$

_____

[5]This choice can be viewed as an extension of the transform presented in [20, 21, 24].

and using (4.26) through (4.29) with (4.24) computed for the finest two scales, we obtain

$$\sum_{i=1}^{I} G_{st}(\omega_r, \omega_\phi - \theta_i) K_{st}(\omega_r, \omega_\phi - \theta_i) + H_{st}(\omega_r) L_{st}(\omega_r) = 1. \tag{4.30}$$

Setting $\hat{\phi}(\omega_r) = \hat{\beta}_p(\omega_r)$, and employing (3.5) and (4.25) with (4.26) and (4.27), we find that

$$H_{st}(\omega_r) = H_{-s}(\omega_r) \tag{4.31}$$

and

$$G_{st}(\omega_r, \omega_\theta) = (\cos(\omega_\theta))^d G_{-s}(\omega_r), \tag{4.32}$$

where $H(\omega)$ and $G(\omega)$ are specified by (3.9) and (3.15), respectively.

By inserting (4.31) and (4.32) into (4.30), the missing two filters can be chosen as

$$L_{st}(\omega_r) = L_s(\omega_r) \tag{4.33}$$

and

$$K_{st}(\omega_r, \omega_\theta) = \frac{1}{C_d} (\cos(\omega_\theta))^d K_s(\omega_r), \tag{4.34}$$

where $L(\omega)$ and $K(\omega)$ are given by (3.16) and (3.17), respectively, and $C_d = \sum_{i=1}^{I} \left(\cos(\omega - \theta_i) \right)^{2d}$.

4.4 Multiscale Spline Derivative-Based Transform

Let us pause here for a brief assessment of the two-dimensional steerable transform derived so far. We have chosen steerable wavelets (4.25) which are equal to d-th order derivatives of circularly symmetric spline functions in the direction of x-axis (note that knots for these splines are circles) and we have laid a foundation for filter bank implementations in (4.30). An obvious shortcoming of this scheme is the fact that none of the filter kernels obtained from (4.31) through (4.34) is compactly supported on the rectangular grid. For implementations using digital filters, one is therefore forced to approximate these frequency responses, and by doing so, (4.30) may not hold anymore. Filters in filter bank implementations of steerable pyramids described in [17, 38, 39], for example, were designed by using various techniques for approximating desired frequency responses. None of the reported filter banks achieved perfect reconstruction and all filter kernels were nonseparable. Here, we will take a different approach. We will approximate the wavelets in (4.25) in a way that will lead to x-y separable filters in a perfect reconstruction filter bank implementation of the transform such that the quality of approximation will improve by increasing the order of B-splines.

Let us approximate wavelets from (4.25) with

$$\psi(x,y) = \frac{d^d \beta_{p+d}(x)}{dx^d} \beta_{p+d}(y). \tag{4.35}$$

Based on the fact that B-splines tend to a Gaussian as their order increases, it is easy to see that both wavelets (4.25) and (4.35) converge to the same functions (i.e., d-th order derivatives of the normalized Gaussian in the direction of x-axis) as $p \to \infty$.

In order to steer wavelets $\psi(x,y)$ given by (4.35) (note that steering will be only approximate, since these wavelets are not steerable), we need to find basis functions that will approximately steer $\psi(x,y)$. Computing rotations, as we did in (4.20), is not practical here, because arbitrary rotations of (4.35) cannot be expressed exactly in terms of central B-spline functions from Chapter 2. Instead, we take advantage of the property of circularly symmetric functions that rotations of their directional derivatives are equal to directional derivatives in rotated directions:

$$\mathcal{R}_{\theta_0} \left\{ \frac{\partial^d \varrho_c(x,y)}{\partial \vec{n}^d} \right\} = \frac{\partial^d \varrho_c(x,y)}{\partial \vec{n}_{\theta_0}^d},$$

where $\mathcal{R}_{\theta_0}$ stands for rotation by θ_0, $\frac{\partial \varrho_c(x,y)}{\partial \vec{n}} = \vec{n} \vec{\nabla} \varrho_c(x,y)$, $\varrho_c(x,y)$ is a circularly symmetric function, and $\vec{n}_{\theta_0}$ denotes vector $\vec{n} = (\cos\theta, \sin\theta)$ rotated by θ_0.

Let us choose

$$\varrho(x,y) = \beta_{p+d}(x)\beta_{p+d}(y),$$

which is approximately circularly symmetric function for higher order splines. A rotation of $\psi(x,y) = \frac{\partial^d \varrho(x,y)}{\partial x^d}$ from (4.35) by θ_0 can therefore be approximated by

$$\psi^{\theta_0}(x,y) \simeq \frac{\partial^d \varrho(x,y)}{\partial \vec{n}^d} = \sum_{i=0}^{d} \binom{d}{i} n_x^{d-i} n_y^i \frac{d^{d-i}\beta_{p+d}(x)}{dx^{d-i}} \frac{d^i \beta_{p+d}(y)}{dy^i}, \qquad (4.36)$$

where $\vec{n} = (\cos\theta_0, \sin\theta_0) = (n_x, n_y)$.

Note that in case of Gaussian, which is both x-y separable and circularly symmetric, (4.36) becomes exact (e.g., for $\varrho(x,y) = e^{-(x^2+y^2)}$, $\theta_0 = -\theta$, and $d = \{2, 4\}$, we obtain, up to a scaling factor, x-y separable basis set for the second and fourth derivative of Gaussian from Tables III and VII of [12]).

Having found a set of basis functions (4.36) that approximately steer wavelets (4.35), we want to construct a transform such that Equations (4.20) through (4.24) will be valid (superscript i must be viewed now as an index, rather than rotation by θ_i). In frequency domain, we can express basis functions from (4.36) as

$$\hat{\psi}^{i+1}(\omega_x, \omega_y) = G_{-s}^{d-i}(\omega_x) G_{-s}^{i}(\omega_y) \hat{\beta}_{p+i}(\omega_x) \hat{\beta}_{p+d-i}(\omega_y), \qquad i = 0, 1, \ldots, d, \qquad (4.37)$$

where $G^d(\omega)$ is given by (3.15) and $G^0(\omega) = 1$.

Choosing appropriate $\hat{\chi}^i(\omega_x, \omega_y)$ to obtain a relation needed for the filter bank implementation of the transform is more complicated than in one dimension. Since we could not find a general solution for arbitrary d, we solve each case separately. Below, we present solutions for the first four orders. When $d \leq 2$, we impose $\hat{\varphi}(\omega_x, \omega_y) = \hat{\phi}(\omega_x, \omega_y) = \hat{\beta}_p(\omega_x)\hat{\beta}_p(\omega_y)$, a constraint analogous to the one from Section 3.1.

For $d = 1$, we write similar to [28]

$$\hat{\chi}^1(\omega_x, \omega_y) = K_s^1(\omega_x) T_1(\omega_y) \hat{\beta}_p(\omega_x) \hat{\beta}_{p-1}(\omega_y), \qquad (4.38)$$

$$\hat{\chi}^2(\omega_x, \omega_y) = T_1(\omega_x) K_s^1(\omega_y) \hat{\beta}_{p-1}(\omega_x) \hat{\beta}_p(\omega_y), \qquad (4.39)$$

where $K^d(\omega)$ and $T_1(\omega)$ are given by (3.17) and (4.11), respectively.

Computing (4.24) for the finest two scales and inserting (3.5), (4.37), (4.38), and (4.39) yields a relation between frequency responses

$$G^1(\omega_x)K^1(\omega_x)T_1(\omega_y) + T_1(\omega_x)G^1(\omega_y)K^1(\omega_y) + |H(\omega_x)H(\omega_y)|^2 = 1.$$

For $d = 2$, we choose

$$\hat{\chi}^1(\omega_x,\omega_y) = K_s^2(\omega_x)T_2(\omega_y)\hat{\beta}_p(\omega_x)\hat{\beta}_{p-2}(\omega_y), \tag{4.40}$$

$$\hat{\chi}^2(\omega_x,\omega_y) = K_s^1(\omega_x)K_s^1(\omega_y)\hat{\beta}_{p-1}(\omega_x)\hat{\beta}_{p-1}(\omega_y), \tag{4.41}$$

$$\hat{\chi}^3(\omega_x,\omega_y) = T_2(\omega_x)K_s^2(\omega_y)\hat{\beta}_{p-2}(\omega_x)\hat{\beta}_p(\omega_y), \tag{4.42}$$

where

$$T_2(\omega) = |H(\omega)|^2. \tag{4.43}$$

Using (3.5), (4.37), and (4.40) through (4.42) with (4.24) results in

$$G^2(\omega_x)K^2(\omega_x)T_2(\omega_y) + G^1(\omega_x)K^1(\omega_x)G^1(\omega_y)K^1(\omega_y) + T_2(\omega_x)G^2(\omega_y)K^2(\omega_y) +$$
$$+ |H(\omega_x)H(\omega_y)|^2 = 1.$$

For orders $d > 2$, we require $\hat{\phi}(\omega_x,\omega_y) = \hat{\beta}_p(\omega_x)\hat{\beta}_p(\omega_y)$ and $\hat{\varphi}(\omega_x,\omega_y) = \hat{\varphi}(\omega_x)\hat{\varphi}(\omega_y)$, where $\hat{\varphi}(\omega)$ is specified by (3.7) and (3.16).

For $d = 3$, we choose reconstructing functions

$$\hat{\chi}^1(\omega_x,\omega_y) = K_s^3(\omega_x)\hat{\varphi}(\omega_x)\hat{\varphi}_{-3}(\omega_y), \tag{4.44}$$

$$\hat{\chi}^2(\omega_x,\omega_y) = -K_s^2(\omega_x)K_s^1(\omega_y)V_3(\omega_x)V_3(\omega_y)\hat{\varphi}_{-1}(\omega_x)\hat{\varphi}_{-2}(\omega_y), \tag{4.45}$$

$$\hat{\chi}^3(\omega_x,\omega_y) = -K_s^1(\omega_x)K_s^2(\omega_y)V_3(\omega_x)V_3(\omega_y)\hat{\varphi}_{-2}(\omega_x)\hat{\varphi}_{-1}(\omega_y), \tag{4.46}$$

$$\hat{\chi}^4(\omega_x,\omega_y) = K_s^3(\omega_y)\hat{\varphi}_{-3}(\omega_x)\hat{\varphi}(\omega_y), \tag{4.47}$$

where

$$V_3(\omega) = \frac{1}{\sqrt{2}}(1 - |H(\omega)|^2), \tag{4.48}$$

and $\hat{\varphi}_{-i}(\omega) \in L^1(\boldsymbol{R})$ denotes a function such that $\hat{\varphi}(\omega) = \hat{\beta}_{i-1}(\omega)\hat{\varphi}_{-i}(\omega)$, $i \in \boldsymbol{N}$.

Employing (4.37), (3.5), (3.7), and (4.44) through (4.47) with (4.24) yields a relation

$$G^3(\omega_x)K^3(\omega_x) - G^2(\omega_x)K^2(\omega_x)V_3(\omega_x)G^1(\omega_y)K^1(\omega_y)V_3(\omega_y) -$$

$$-G^1(\omega_x)K^1(\omega_x)V_3(\omega_x)G^2(\omega_y)K^2(\omega_y)V_3(\omega_y) + G^3(\omega_y)K^3(\omega_y) +$$

$$+H(\omega_x)L(\omega_x)H(\omega_y)L(\omega_y) = 1,$$

where $L(\omega)$ is specified by (3.16).

For $d = 4$, our choices are

$$\hat{\chi}^1(\omega_x,\omega_y) = K_s^4(\omega_x)T_2(\omega_y)\hat{\varphi}(\omega_x)\hat{\varphi}_{-4}(\omega_y), \qquad (4.49)$$

$$\hat{\chi}^2(\omega_x,\omega_y) = K_s^3(\omega_x)K_s^1(\omega_y)\hat{\varphi}_{-1}(\omega_x)\hat{\varphi}_{-3}(\omega_y), \qquad (4.50)$$

$$\hat{\chi}^3(\omega_x,\omega_y) = -K_s^2(\omega_x)K_s^2(\omega_y)V_4(\omega_x)V_4(\omega_y)\hat{\varphi}_{-2}(\omega_x)\hat{\varphi}_{-2}(\omega_y), \qquad (4.51)$$

$$\hat{\chi}^4(\omega_x,\omega_y) = K_s^1(\omega_x)K_s^3(\omega_y)\hat{\varphi}_{-3}(\omega_x)\hat{\varphi}_{-1}(\omega_y), \qquad (4.52)$$

$$\hat{\chi}^5(\omega_x,\omega_y) = T_2(\omega_x)K_s^4(\omega_y)\hat{\varphi}_{-4}(\omega_x)\hat{\varphi}(\omega_y), \qquad (4.53)$$

where

$$V_4(\omega_x) = 1 - |H(\omega)|^2. \qquad (4.54)$$

Using the above functions (4.49) through (4.53), (4.37), (3.5), and (3.7) in (4.24) computed for the finest two scales gives

$$G^4(\omega_x)K^4(\omega_x)T_2(\omega_y) + G^3(\omega_x)K^3(\omega_x)G^1(\omega_y)K^1(\omega_y) -$$

$$-G^2(\omega_x)K^2(\omega_x)V_4(\omega_x)G^2(\omega_y)K^2(\omega_y)V_4(\omega_y) + G^1(\omega_x)K^1(\omega_x)G^3(\omega_y)K^3(\omega_y) +$$

$$+T_2(\omega_x)G^4(\omega_y)K^4(\omega_y) + H(\omega_x)L(\omega_x)H(\omega_y)L(\omega_y) = 1.$$

Here, we have even more freedom for choosing the reconstructing functions than in one dimension. The above functions for $d = \{2,3,4\}$ were found by trying to imitate the one-dimensional transform from Chapter 3 as much as possible. All decomposition filters $G^d(\omega)$ were first paired with corresponding reconstruction filters

$K^d(\omega)$, and then all other potential digital filters were specified as polynomials in $H_{-s}(\omega)$. We inserted thus specified filters into a relation between their frequency responses and solved for the unknown polynomial coefficients. Since we allowed more filters with higher-degree polynomials than expected in the solution, the resulting system of linear equations was underdetermined. This allowed enough freedom for removal of undesired digital filters and for balance between degrees of polynomials.

The described procedure for determination of reconstructing functions and filters involves quite a lot of heuristics to obtain the appropriate solution from the underdetermined linear system. Unfortunately, we are not aware of any systematic way (aside from numerical optimization, which may be pretty cumbersome) to obtain solutions comparable to the ones above.

Next, we will derive a filter bank implementation of the transform. As in Section 4.1, we assume a bandlimited input signal: $\hat{s}(\omega_x, \omega_y) = 0$ for $|\omega_x| > \pi$ or $|\omega_y| > \pi$. Using Shannon's sampling theorem in two dimensions [16] with (4.20) and basis functions from (4.37), we can write

$$W_0^i s(x, y) = \int_{-\infty}^{\infty} \int_{-\infty}^{\infty} \sum_{i_x=-\infty}^{\infty} \sum_{i_y=-\infty}^{\infty} s(i_x, i_y) \operatorname{sinc}(t_x - i_x) \operatorname{sinc}(t_y - i_y) \cdot$$

$$\cdot \sum_{m_x=-\infty}^{\infty} g_{-s}^{d-i}(m_x) \beta_{p+i}(x - t_x - m_x) \sum_{m_y=-\infty}^{\infty} g_{-s}^i(m_y) \beta_{p+d-i}(y - t_y - m_y)\, dt_x\, dt_y,$$

where $i = 0, 1, \ldots, d$ as in (4.37).

Again, we approximate sinc functions with r-order cardinal splines, then use (2.4), and get

$$\mathrm{DFT}\{W_m^i s(x, y)\big|_{x=n_x, y=n_y}\} \simeq S(\omega_x, \omega_y)\, B_r^{-1}(\omega_x)\, B_r^{-1}(\omega_y)\, B_{p+r+i+1}(\omega_x) \cdot$$

$$\cdot B_{p+r+d-i+1}(\omega_y)\, G_{-s}^{d-i}(2^m \omega_x)\, G_{-s}^i(2^m \omega_y) \prod_{n=0}^{m-1} H_{-s}^{p+i}(2^n \omega_x) H_{-s}^{p+d-i}(2^n \omega_y). \quad (4.55)$$

Using (4.55) with an approximation $B_{p+r+i+1}(\omega) \simeq B_{p+r}(\omega) B_i(\omega)$, we can obtain a filter bank implementation of the transform decomposition. The reconstruction part follows from (4.24), (4.37), and reconstructing functions for distinct values of d.

Figure 4.2 shows filter bank implementations of a multiscale spline derivative-based transform for $d = \{1, 2, 3, 4\}$. For $d = 1$, we recognize (except for the prefiltering and postfiltering) the filter bank implementation of a two-dimensional discrete dyadic wavelet transform from [28]. For $d = 2$, however, our transform differs from the filter bank presented in [22] (i.e., the corresponding transform described in Section 4.1): second derivative is computed only in the directions of x and y-axis in [18, 22], which is not enough for steering. Although not particularly appropriate for orientation analysis, such a scheme may still, as we have seen in Section 4.1, efficiently approximate Laplacian of Gaussian across dyadic scales.

A transform similar to the one described in this section, was presented in [17, 38, 39]. Their filter bank implementation is less redundant (downsampling is used on the lowpass branch, while simultaneously keeping aliasing negligible by using a filter with insignificant amount of energy for $|\omega_r| > \frac{\pi}{2}$) and uses reconstruction filters with same magnitude frequency responses as the decomposition ones—a possible advantage for certain applications. They have, on the other hand, little control over the function from which derivatives are computed (to obtain a d-th derivative, they multiply a circularly symmetric filter by $(-j \cos \theta)^d$ with all filters being obtained by recursive minimization of a weighted combination of constraints), filter bank does not have perfect reconstruction, and none of the filters is x-y separable.

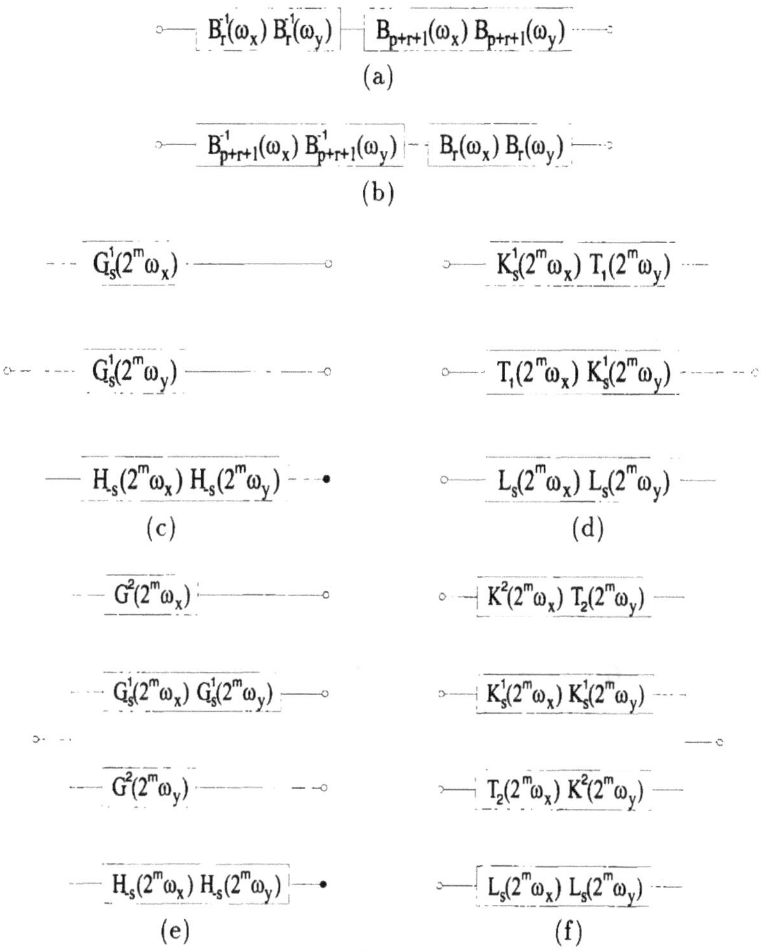

$B_r^1(\omega_x)\, B_r^1(\omega_y)$ | $B_{p+r+1}(\omega_x)\, B_{p+r+1}(\omega_y)$

(a)

$\overline{B_{p+r+1}^{-1}(\omega_x)\, B_{p+r+1}^{-1}(\omega_y)}$ | $B_r(\omega_x)\, B_r(\omega_y)$

(b)

$\overline{G_s^1(2^m\omega_x)}$ $\overline{K_s^1(2^m\omega_x)\, T_1(2^m\omega_y)}$

$\overline{G_s^1(2^m\omega_y)}$ $\overline{T_1(2^m\omega_x)\, K_s^1(2^m\omega_y)}$

$\overline{H_s(2^m\omega_x)\, H_s(2^m\omega_y)}$ $\overline{L_s(2^m\omega_x)\, L_s(2^m\omega_y)}$

(c)   (d)

$\overline{G^2(2^m\omega_x)}$ $\overline{K^2(2^m\omega_x)\, T_2(2^m\omega_y)}$

$\overline{G_s^1(2^m\omega_x)\, G_s^1(2^m\omega_y)}$ $\overline{K_s^1(2^m\omega_x)\, K_s^1(2^m\omega_y)}$

$\overline{G^2(2^m\omega_y)}$ $\overline{T_2(2^m\omega_x)\, K^2(2^m\omega_y)}$

$\overline{H_s(2^m\omega_x)\, H_s(2^m\omega_y)}$ $\overline{L_s(2^m\omega_x)\, L_s(2^m\omega_y)}$

(e)   (f)

Figure 4.2: Filter bank implementation of a multiscale spline derivative-based transform for $m \in [0, M-1]$: (a) Prefiltering, (b) postfiltering, (c) decomposition and (d) reconstruction modules for $d = 1$, and (e) decomposition and (f) reconstruction modules for $d = 2$.

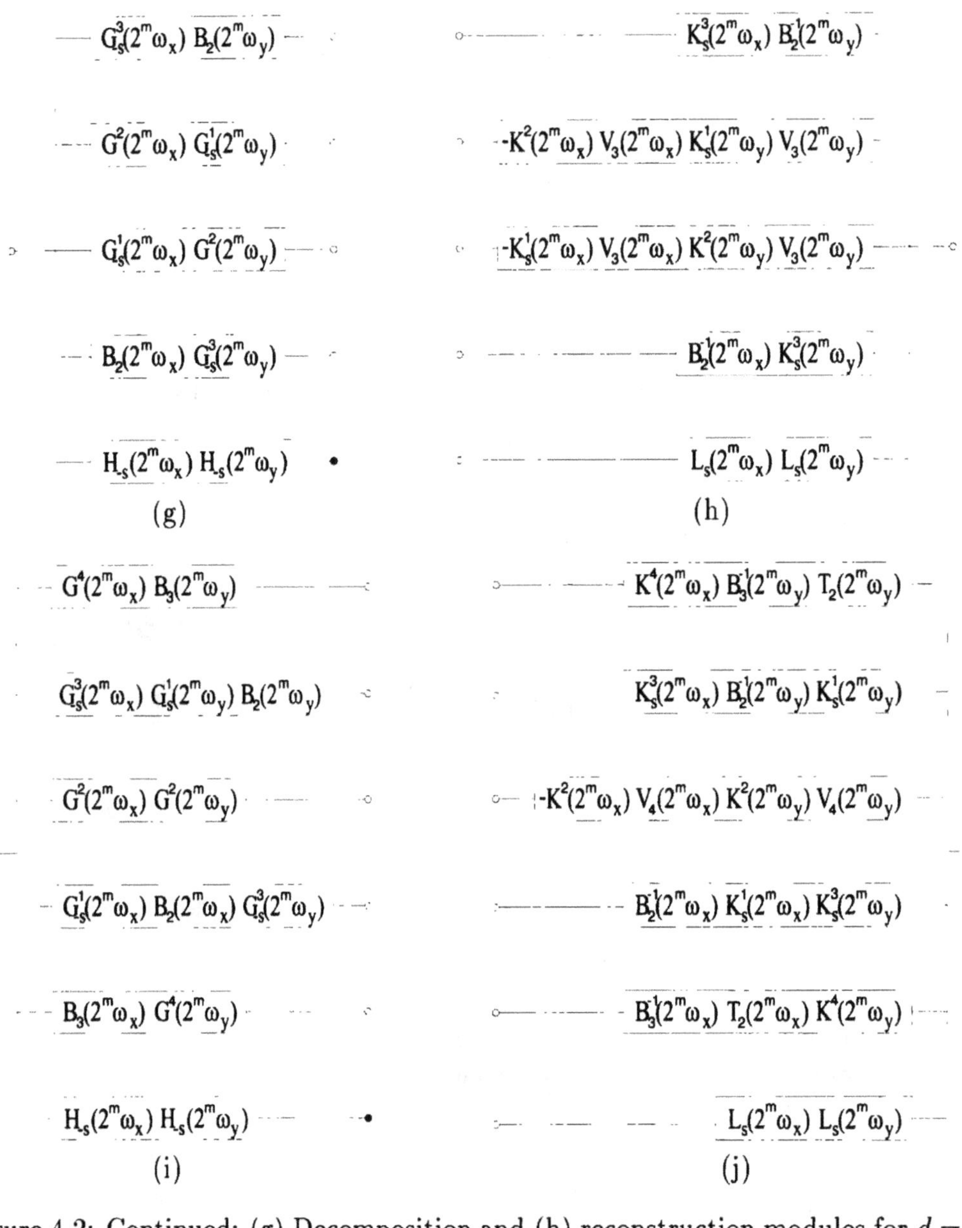

— $G_s^3(2^m\omega_x)\ B_2(2^m\omega_y)$ —

$G^2(2^m\omega_x)\ G_s^1(2^m\omega_y)$

— $G_s^1(2^m\omega_x)\ G^2(2^m\omega_y)$ —

— $B_2(2^m\omega_x)\ G_s^3(2^m\omega_y)$ —

— $H_s(2^m\omega_x)\ H_s(2^m\omega_y)$ •

(g)

$G^4(2^m\omega_x)\ B_3(2^m\omega_y)$

$G_s^3(2^m\omega_x)\ G_s^1(2^m\omega_y)\ B_2(2^m\omega_y)$

$G^2(2^m\omega_x)\ G^2(2^m\omega_y)$

$G_s^1(2^m\omega_x)\ B_2(2^m\omega_x)\ G_s^3(2^m\omega_y)$

$B_3(2^m\omega_x)\ G^4(2^m\omega_y)$

$H_s(2^m\omega_x)\ H_s(2^m\omega_y)$ •

(i)

$K_s^3(2^m\omega_x)\ B_2(2^m\omega_y)$

$K^2(2^m\omega_x)\ V_3(2^m\omega_x)\ K_s^1(2^m\omega_y)\ V_3(2^m\omega_y)$

$K_s^1(2^m\omega_x)\ V_3(2^m\omega_x)\ K^2(2^m\omega_y)\ V_3(2^m\omega_y)$

$B_2(2^m\omega_x)\ K_s^3(2^m\omega_y)$

$L_s(2^m\omega_x)\ L_s(2^m\omega_y)$

(h)

$K^4(2^m\omega_x)\ B_3(2^m\omega_y)\ T_2(2^m\omega_y)$

$K_s^3(2^m\omega_x)\ B_2(2^m\omega_y)\ K_s^1(2^m\omega_y)$

$K^2(2^m\omega_x)\ V_4(2^m\omega_x)\ K^2(2^m\omega_y)\ V_4(2^m\omega_y)$

$B_2(2^m\omega_x)\ K_s^1(2^m\omega_x)\ K_s^3(2^m\omega_y)$

$B_3(2^m\omega_x)\ T_2(2^m\omega_x)\ K^4(2^m\omega_y)$

$L_s(2^m\omega_x)\ L_s(2^m\omega_y)$

(j)

Figure 4.2: Continued: (g) Decomposition and (h) reconstruction modules for $d = 3$, and (i) decomposition and (j) reconstruction modules for $d = 4$. Decomposition modules are recursively applied at the locations of the filled circles.

CHAPTER 5
IMPLEMENTATION ISSUES

Except for the steerable dyadic wavelet transform, all transforms presented in Chapters 3 and 4 can be implemented as filter banks consisting of one-dimensional filters only. In this chapter, we show how to take advantage of symmetry/antisymmetry of filters when combined with a mirror extended input signal.

5.1   Finite Impulse Response Filters

Since all two-dimensional filters used in the filter bank implementations of the transforms from Chapter 4 are x-y separable, we will begin this section with a detailed description of FIR filter implementations for the one-dimensional discrete dyadic wavelet transform implementation from Figure 3.1. The extension to two dimensions will then be straightforward.

Let us refer to filters applied at scale 2^m as filters at level $m+1$, and let filters at level 1 (Equations (3.9), (3.15) through (3.17), (4.11), (4.43), (4.48), and (4.54)) be called "original filters," to distinguish them from their upsampled versions. As an input to the filter bank from Figure 3.1, we consider a real signal $s(n) \in l^2(\mathbf{Z})$, $n \in [0, N-1]$. Depending on the length of each filter impulse response, filtering an input signal may be computed either by multiplying the discrete Fourier transforms of the two sequences or by circularly convolving $s(n)$ with a filter's impulse response.[1] Of course, such a periodically extended signal may change abruptly at the boundaries causing artifacts. A common remedy for such a problem is realized by constructing

---

[1] As is customary in image processing, we use circular, rather than linear, convolution.

a mirror extended signal [18]

$$s_{me}(n) = \begin{cases} s(-n-1) & \text{if } n \in [-N, -1] \\ s(n) & \text{if } n \in [0, N-1], \end{cases} \qquad (5.1)$$

where we chose the signal $s_{me}(n)$ to be supported in $[-N, N-1]$. It will become evident shortly, that mirror extension is particularly elegant in conjunction with symmetric/antisymmetric filters.

Let us first classify symmetric/antisymmetric real even-length signals into four types [30]:

Type I $f(n) = f(-n)$,

Type II $f(n) = f(-n-1)$,

Type III $f(n) = -f(-n)$,

Type IV $f(n) = -f(-n-1)$,

where $n \in [-N, N-1]$. Note that for Type I signals the values at $f(0)$ and $f(-N)$ are unique, and that for Type III signals the values at $f(0)$ and $f(-N)$ are equal to zero.

Using properties of the Fourier transform it is easy to show that the convolution of symmetric/antisymmetric real signals results in a symmetric/antisymmetric real signal. If a symmetric/antisymmetric real signal has an even length, then there always exists an integer shift such that the shifted signal belongs to one of the above types.

Now, we are ready to examine the filter bank implementation of a one-dimensional discrete dyadic wavelet transform from Figure 3.1 with filters given by (3.9) and (3.15) through (3.17) driven by a mirrored signal $s_{me}(n)$ at the input. Let the number of levels M be restricted by

$$M \leq 1 + \log_2 \frac{N-1}{L_{max}-1}, \qquad (5.2)$$

where L_{max} is the length of the longest original FIR filter impulse response.

Each FIR filter block in the filter bank consists of a filter and a circular shift operator. Equation (5.2) guarantees that the length of the filter impulse response does not exceed the length of the signal at any block.

Since our input signal $s_{me}(n)$ is of Type II and noninteger shifts at level 1 are rounded to the nearest integer, it follows that a processed signal at any point in the filter bank belongs to one of the types defined above. This means that filtering a signal of length $2N$ can be reduced to filtering a signal of approximately one half of its length. (For Types I and III, $N + 1$ samples are needed. However. for Type III one needs to store only $N - 1$ values because zero values are always present at the zeroth and $(-N)$-th sample position).

Implementation is particularly simple for FIR filters designed with d even and p odd. Filters are of Type I in this case, so the signal at any point of the filter bank will be of Type II. An FIR filter block from the filter bank shown in Figure 3.1 can therefore be implemented by

$$F_{s,m}u(n) = f(0)u_{II}(n) + \sum_{i=1}^{\frac{L-1}{2}} f(i)[u_{II}(n - 2^m i) + u_{II}(n + 2^m i)], \quad n \in [0, N-1], \quad (5.3)$$

where

$$u_{II}(n) = \begin{cases} u(-n - 1) & \text{if } n \in [-\frac{N}{2}, -1] \\ u(n) & \text{if } n \in [0, N - 1] \\ u(2N - n - 1) & \text{if } n \in [N, \frac{3N}{2}], \end{cases} \quad (5.4)$$

$u(n)$ is an input signal to a block, $f(n)$ is an impulse response of some original filter, L is the length of the filter, and N is the length of an input signal $s(n)$ to the filter bank. Implementation of filters $b_p(n)$ used for prefiltering and postfiltering represents a special case of (5.3) with $m = 0$.

A filter bank with the above implementation of blocks and signal $s(n)$ at the input yields equivalent results as circular convolution for $s_{me}(n)$ as defined by (5.1). In addition to requiring one half the amount of memory, the computational savings over a circular convolution implementation of blocks are, depending on the original filter length, three to four times fewer multiplications and one half as many additions.

A similar approach can be used for other filters. However, things get slightly more complicated in this case, because the filters are not of the same type and the signal components within the filter bank are of distinct types. As a consequence, an implementation of blocks that use distinct original filters may not be the same, and the implementation of blocks at level 1 may differ from the implementation of blocks at other levels of analysis.

The decomposition blocks at level 1 can be implemented by

$$G_{-s,0}u(n) = \sum_{i=0}^{\frac{L}{2}-1} g(i)[u_{II}(n-i-1) - u_{II}(n+i)], \quad n \in [1, N-1],$$

for d odd, (5.3) for d even,

$$H_{-s,0}u(n) = \sum_{i=0}^{\frac{L}{2}-1} h(i)[u_{II}(n-i-1) + u_{II}(n+i)], \quad n \in [0, N],$$

for p even, and (5.3) for p odd, where $u_{II}(l)$ is defined by (5.4), $g(n)$ and $h(n)$ are impulse responses of the filters computed from (3.15) and (3.9), respectively, and L is the length of the corresponding impulse response.

The output from a block $G_{-s}(\omega)$ at level 1 is of Type III for d odd and of Type II for d even, while the output from $H_{-s}(\omega)$ at the same level is of Type I for p even and of Type II for p odd.

The decomposition blocks at subsequent levels $m \in [1, M-1]$ can be implemented by

$$G_{-s,m}u(n) = \sum_{i=0}^{\frac{L}{2}-1} g(i)[u_I(n-2^m(i+s)) - u_I(n+2^m(i+s))], \quad n \in [1, N-1],$$

for d odd and p even,

$$G_{-s,m}u(n) = \sum_{i=0}^{\frac{L}{2}-1} g(i)[u_{II}(n-2^m(i+s)) - u_{II}(n+2^m(i+s))], \quad n \in [0, N-1],$$

for d and p odd,

$$F_{-s,m}u(n) = f(0)u_I(n) + \sum_{i=1}^{\frac{L-1}{2}} f(i)[u_I(n - 2^m i) + u_I(n + 2^m i)], \quad n \in [0, N], \quad (5.5)$$

with $f(n) = g(n)$ for d and p even,

$$H_{-s,m}u(n) = \sum_{i=0}^{\frac{L}{2}-1} h(i)[u_I(n - 2^m(i + s)) + u_I(n + 2^m(i + s))], \quad n \in [0, N], \quad (5.6)$$

for p even, and (5.3) for p odd, where

$$u_I(n) = \begin{cases} u(-n) & \text{if } n \in [-\frac{N}{2}, -1] \\ u(n) & \text{if } n \in [0, N] \\ u(2N - n) & \text{if } n \in [N + 1, \frac{3N}{2}]. \end{cases} \quad (5.7)$$

The outputs from blocks $G_{-s}(2^m\omega)$ are of Type III for d odd and p even, of Type IV for d and p odd, and of Type I for d and p even, whereas the outputs from $H_{-s}(2^m\omega)$ are of Type I for p even and of Type II for p odd.

Next, the reconstruction blocks at level 1 can be implemented by

$$K_{s,0}u(n) = \sum_{i=1}^{\frac{L}{2}} k(i)[u_{III}(n - i + 1) - u_{III}(n + i)], \quad n \in [0, N - 1],$$

for d odd, (5.3) for d even,

$$L_{s,0}u(n) = \sum_{i=1}^{\frac{L}{2}} l(i)[u_I(n - i + 1) + u_I(n + i)], \quad n \in [0, N - 1],$$

for p even, and (5.3) for p odd, where

$$u_{III}(n) = \begin{cases} -u(-n) & \text{if } n \in [-\frac{N}{2}, -1] \\ 0 & \text{if } n = 0 \\ u(n) & \text{if } n \in [1, N - 1] \\ 0 & \text{if } n = N \\ -u(2N - n) & \text{if } n \in [N + 1, \frac{3N}{2}], \end{cases} \quad (5.8)$$

$u_I(n)$ is as defined by (5.7) and $k(n)$ is an impulse response of the filter from (3.17). Note that both outputs from blocks $K_s(\omega)$ and $L_s(\omega)$ are of Type II.

The reconstruction blocks at subsequent levels can be implemented by

$$K_{s,m}u(n) = \sum_{i=0}^{\frac{L}{2}-1} k(i + 1)[u_{III}(n - 2^m(i + s)) - u_{III}(n + 2^m(i + s))], \quad n \in [0, N],$$

for d odd and p even, (5.5) with $f(n) = k(n)$ for d and p even,

$$K_{s,m}u(n) = \sum_{i=0}^{\frac{L}{2}-1} k(i+1)[u_{IV}(n-2^m(i+s)) - u_{IV}(n+2^m(i+s))], \qquad n \in [0, N-1],$$

for d and p odd,

$$L_{s,m}u(n) = H_{-s,m}u(n),$$

for p even, and (5.3) for p odd, where $u_{III}(l)$ is given by (5.8),

$$u_{IV}(n) = \begin{cases} -u(-n-1) & \text{if } n \in [-\frac{N}{2}, -1] \\ u(n) & \text{if } n \in [0, N-1] \\ -u(2N-n-1) & \text{if } n \in [N, \frac{3N}{2}], \end{cases}$$

and $H_{-s,m}u(n)$ is specified by (5.6). We observe that the outputs from blocks $K_s(2^m\omega)$ and $L_s(2^m\omega)$, $m \in [1, M-1]$, are of Type I for p even, and of Type II for p odd.

When we compare the above implementation of blocks to circular convolution driven by a mirrored signal $s_{me}(n)$ at the input, we observe that approximately twofold less memory space, three to four times fewer multiplications and one half as many additions are required. (For Type I signals an additional sample has to be saved because two values are without a pair).

Until now, we have talked only about the one-dimensional case, whose filter bank implementation is depicted in Figure 4.2. Two-dimensional transform filter bank implementations (Figures 4.1 and 4.2) are not only comprised of x-y separable filters solely, but also use all the filters from Section 3.1. Everything presented in this section so far is therefore directly applicable to the two-dimensional case. Filters which have not been treated yet (i.e., $t_1(n)$, $t_2(n)$, $v_3(n)$, $v_4(n)$, and filters $b_p(n)$ from the decomposition modules of Figure 4.2) can all be realized by (5.3) for p odd or $m = 0$ and (5.5) otherwise ($f(n)$ denotes an impulse response of any of the above mentioned zero-phase filters in this case).[2]

---

[2] In case of filters $v_3(n)$ and $v_4(n)$, a slightly more efficient implementation can be obtained by precomputing new filters $k * v_3(n)$ and $k * v_4(n)$, and then implementing them by $K_{s,m}u(n)$, $m \in [0, M-1]$.

The implementation presented in this section performs all operations in the spatial domain, however, one could also implement the structures shown in Figures 3.1, 4.1, and 4.2 with an input signal $s_{me}(n)$ (Equation (5.1)) in the frequency domain. For short filter impulse responses, such as those given in Tables 3.1, 3.2 and 3.3, the spatial implementation described in this section is certainly more efficient. For long filter impulse responses, however, filtering is faster if implemented in the frequency domain. Additional details on alternative implementation strategies can be found in [33].

5.2   Infinite Impulse Response Filters

Implementation of IIR filters $b_p^{-1}(n)$ which were introduced in Section 2.2 is a bit more involved than the one encountered in the previous section. Fortunately, the number of different cases is much smaller here: possible input to $b_p^{-1}(n)$ in filter banks from Figures 3.1, 4.1, and 4.2 is either of Type II or of Type I.[3] We will use ideas and a few results from [43].

Let us first take a closer look at the system function $B_p^{-1}(z)$. This function can be written as a cascade of terms

$$E(z) = \frac{1}{z - \frac{1+\alpha^2}{\alpha} + z^{-1}} = \frac{-\alpha}{(1 - \alpha z^{-1})(1 - \alpha z)}, \qquad (5.9)$$

which can be expressed in a parallel form as

$$E(z) = \frac{-\alpha}{1 - \alpha^2} \left(\frac{1}{1 - \alpha z^{-1}} + \frac{1}{1 - \alpha z} - 1 \right), \qquad (5.10)$$

where α and $\frac{1}{\alpha}$ are poles of the causal and the anticausal filter, respectively.

The impulse response of this term can be written as

$$e(n) = \frac{-\alpha}{1 - \alpha^2} \alpha^{|n|}.$$

---

[3]Note that symmetry types in this section slightly differ from those defined in Section 5.1: here, mirror extended signals are periodically repeated, so that they stretch from $-\infty$ to ∞.

We choose to implement $E(z)$ in a cascade form and therefore extract the difference equations from (5.9):

$$c^+(n) = u(n) + \alpha\, c^+(n-1) \quad n = 1, 2, \ldots, N-1, \tag{5.11}$$

and

$$c(n) = \alpha\,(c(n+1) - c^+(n)) \quad n = N-2, N-3, \ldots, 0, \tag{5.12}$$

where $u(n)$ denotes the input to the block, $c^+(n)$ is the output from the causal part, and $c(n)$ stands for the output from the block.

To solve (5.11) and (5.12) we need boundary conditions $c^+(0)$ and $c(N-1)$. Let us begin with filters $b_p^{-1}(n)$ in filter bank implementations from Figures 3.1, 4.1, 4.2(a), 4.2(b), and Figures 4.2(h) and 4.2(j) with $m=0$. We derive

$$c^+(0) = \sum_{i=-\infty}^{0} \alpha^{-i} u_{IIp}(i) = u(0) + \sum_{i=0}^{N-1} \frac{\alpha^{i+1} + \alpha^{2N-i}}{1 - \alpha^{2N}} u(i) \simeq u(0) + \sum_{i=0}^{i_0} \alpha^{i+1} u(i), \tag{5.13}$$

and, using parallel form (5.10)

$$c(N-1) = \frac{-\alpha}{1-\alpha^2}(c^+(N-1) + \sum_{i=0}^{N-1} \frac{\alpha^{N-i} + \alpha^{N+1+i}}{1-\alpha^{2N}} u(i)) \simeq$$

$$\simeq \frac{-\alpha}{1-\alpha^2}(c^+(N-1) + \sum_{i=N-1-i_0}^{N-1} \alpha^{N-i} u(i)), \tag{5.14}$$

where

$$u_{IIp}(n) = \begin{cases} u_{II}(n \bmod (2N)) & \text{if } n \geq 0 \\ u_{II}(-(n+1) \bmod (2N)) & \text{if } n < 0, \end{cases}$$

$$u_{II}(n) = \begin{cases} u(n) & \text{if } n \in [0, N-1] \\ u(2N - n - 1) & \text{if } n \in [N, 2N-1], \end{cases}$$

N is the length of an input signal to the filter bank, and $i_0 < N-1$ is selected such that α^{i_0} falls below a predefined precision threshold.

For IIR filters from Figures 4.2(h) and 4.2(j) with $m \in [1, M-1]$ and p odd, we get

$$c^+(0) = \sum_{i=-\infty}^{0} \left[\alpha^{-\frac{i}{2^m}} u_{IIp}(i)\right]_u =$$

$$= u(0) + \sum_{n=0}^{\infty} \sum_{i=0}^{N-1} \left\{ \left[\alpha^{\frac{i+1+2Nn}{2^m}}\right]_u + \left[\alpha^{\frac{2N(n+1)-i}{2^m}}\right]_u \right\} u(i) \tag{5.15}$$

and

$$c(N-1) = \frac{-\alpha}{1-\alpha^2}(c^+(N-1) + \sum_{n=0}^{\infty} \sum_{i=0}^{N-1} \left\{ \left[\alpha^{\frac{N-i+2Nn}{2^m}} \right]_u + \left[\alpha^{\frac{N+1+i+2Nn}{2^m}} \right]_u \right\} u(i), \quad (5.16)$$

where

$$[\alpha^x]_u = \begin{cases} \alpha^x & \text{if } x \in \mathbf{Z} \\ 0 & \text{otherwise.} \end{cases}$$

If N is a power of two and $2^{m-1} \le N$ ((5.2) guarantees that the latter condition is always true) (5.15) becomes

$$c^+(0) = u(0) + \sum_{i=0}^{N-1} \frac{\left[\alpha^{\frac{i+1}{2^m}} \right]_u + \left[\alpha^{\frac{2N-i}{2^m}} \right]_u}{1 - \alpha^{\frac{2N}{2^m}}} u(i),$$

while (5.16) can be written as

$$c(N-1) = \frac{-\alpha}{1-\alpha^2}(c^+(N-1) + \sum_{i=0}^{N-1} \frac{\left[\alpha^{\frac{N-i}{2^m}} \right]_u + \left[\alpha^{\frac{N+1+i}{2^m}} \right]_u}{1 - \alpha^{\frac{2N}{2^m}}} u(i).$$

Finally, the boundary conditions for filters $b_p^{-1}(n)$ from Figures 4.2(h) and 4.2(j) with $m \in [1, M-1]$ and p even are

$$c^+(0) = \sum_{i=-\infty}^{0} \left[\alpha^{-\frac{i}{2^m}} u_{Ip}(i) \right]_u =$$

$$= \sum_{n=0}^{\infty} \left\{ \left[\alpha^{\frac{2Nn}{2^m}} \right]_u u(0) + \left[\alpha^{\frac{N(2n+1)}{2^m}} \right]_u u(N) + \right.$$

$$\left. + \sum_{i=1}^{N-1} \left\{ \left[\alpha^{\frac{i+2Nn}{2^m}} \right]_u + \left[\alpha^{\frac{2N(n+1)-i}{2^m}} \right]_u \right\} u(i) \right\} \quad (5.17)$$

and

$$c(N) = \frac{-\alpha}{1-\alpha^2}(2c^+(N) - u(N)),$$

where

$$u_{Ip}(n) = u_I(|n| \bmod (2N)),$$

$$u_I(n) = \begin{cases} u(n) & \text{if } n \in [0, N] \\ u(2N-n) & \text{if } n \in [N+1, 2N-1], \end{cases}$$

and $c^-(N) = c^+(N)$ with $c^-(n)$ denoting response of the anticausal filter from (5.10) was used.

Again, if N is a power of two and $2^{m-1} \leq N$, (5.17) can be simplified

$$c^+(0) = \frac{u(0) + \alpha^{\frac{N}{2^m}} u(N) + \sum_{i=1}^{N-1} \left\{ \left[\alpha^{\frac{i}{2^m}} \right]_u + \left[\alpha^{\frac{2N-i}{2^m}} \right]_u \right\} u(i)}{1 - \alpha^{\frac{2N}{2^m}}}.$$

Series in expressions for $c^+(0)$, $c(N-1)$, and $c(N)$ for filters from Figures 4.2(h) and 4.2(j) with $m \in [1, M-1]$ can be, similar to (5.13) and (5.14), truncated according to the desired precision.

For orders p greater than three, we implement $B_p^{-1}(z)$ as a cascade of terms $E(z)$ with different α's. Note that the output from block $E(z)$ is always of the same type as the input to it.

CHAPTER 6
APPLICATIONS

In this chapter, we present a comparison between multiscale spline derivative-based transform and traditional wavelet techniques on two sample applications.

6.1   Image Fusion

Image fusion combines particular aspects of information from the same imaging modality or from distinct imaging modalities and can be used to improve the reliability of a particular computational vision task or to provide a human observer with a deeper insight about the nature of observed data. Whether it is combining different sensors or extending the dynamic range of a single sensor, the goal is to achieve more accurate inferences that can be achieved by a single sensor or a single sensor setting.

The simplest method of fusing images is accomplished by computing their average. Such a technique does combine features from input images in the fused image, however, the contrast of the original features can be significantly reduced. Among more sophisticated methods, multiscale and multiresolution analyses have become particularly popular. Different pyramids [5, 41] and wavelet-based techniques [7, 20, 26, 32] have been applied to this problem. Fusion is performed in the transform space by computing local statistics across the decomposition scales. Typical size of neighborhood is between a single pixel and 5×5 area with some loss of contrast reported for the latter [5]. Some authors argue about of the particular criteria for fusion [5, 26], while others propose a set of different combination rules to perform image fusion in a variety of ways [7].

59

Here, we are not trying to find the best criteria for fusion. We simply use a "maximum magnitude" rule (i.e., at each position and scale of the transform the corresponding transform coefficients are compared and those with greater magnitude included for reconstruction) and compare the results obtained by traditional wavelet techniques with the ones produced by the multiscale spline derivative-based transform.

Figure 6.1(a),(b) shows a pair of images with distinct (lower in Figure 6.1(a) and upper in Figure 6.1(b)) areas blurred. Figure 6.1(c) demonstrates the ideal result of image fusion obtained by manually cutting and pasting the upper part of Figure 6.1(a) and the lower part of Figure 6.1(b). Image fusion resulting from the use of discrete wavelet transforms is shown in Figure 6.1(d) for the orthogonal wavelet DAUB12 [7] and in Figure 6.1(e) for the linear phase biorthogonal wavelet Bior6.8. Figure 6.1(f) illustrates the result of image fusion with a multiscale spline derivative-based transform being employed. Note that the image fused using the multiscale spline derivative-based transform is virtually indistinguishable from the one obtained manually. Both orthogonal and biorthogonal wavelet transform exhibit artifacts. On the average, biorthogonal transform performs better than orthogonal due to the linear phase of wavelets and filters, but still causes serious artifacts.

Basing the decision rule on an area rather than on a single pixel certainly reduces artifacts of traditional wavelet methods, however, it reduces sharpness as well. As noted by Burt and Kolczynski [5], "there is a tradeoff between sharpness and shift invariance." Here, we argue the point that the proper choice of transform can eliminate artifacts due to translation and rotation invariance altogether.

Another possible source of artifacts is misregistration. Low-level fusion algorithms typically require input images that have already been properly aligned. Misregistration causes artifacts [7], and it can be recognized from our discussion in Section 1.1 that they are more obvious for translation and rotation-noninvariant wavelet techniques than for the multiscale spline derivative-based transform.

6.2 Image Enhancement

Similar to the previous section, we will point out problems associated with traditional wavelet analysis on an example. Below, we briefly present the problem of contrast enhancement in digital mammography.

In mammography, early detection of breast cancer relies upon the ability to distinguish between malignant and benign mammographic features. Contrast enhancement can make more obvious unseen or barely seen features of a mammogram without requiring additional radiation. The complexity of mammographic images and the subtlety of malignancies can present a challenge even to expert radiologists. In addition to dealing with barely visible mammographic features, human observers sometimes simply overlook abnormalities. Such mistakes affect the number of false-negative cases considerably. Computer processing of digital mammograms can assist radiologists to reach a correct diagnosis more consistently. A variety of computer based techniques have been reported in almost three decades of research. The advent of direct digital mammography devices has made digital image processing techniques more attractive for screening.

Contrast enhancement in a wavelet transform framework can be achieved by applying a (typically nonlinear) function to wavelet coefficients and then reconstructing an enhanced image with modified coefficients. We are not trying to find the best method for a specific type of images or noise here, rather we want to illustrate possible sources of artifacts when orthogonal and biorthogonal wavelet transforms are used.

Figure 6.2(a) shows an original mammographic image. Figure 6.2(b) depicts the result of enhancement using piecewise linear enhancement function [11, 23] to

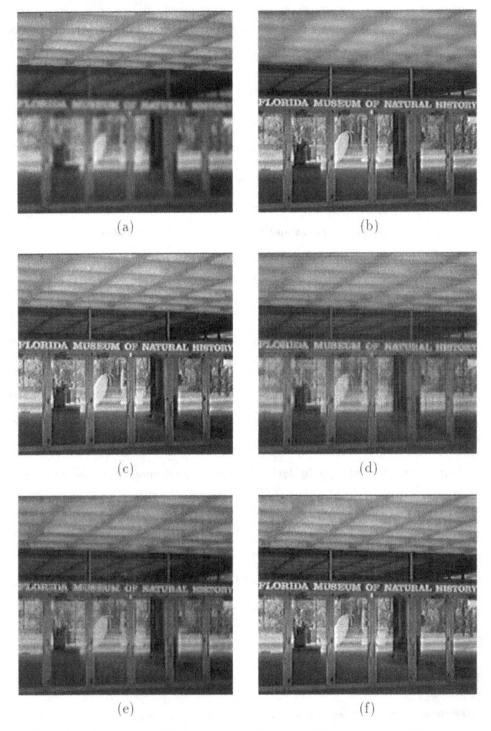

Figure 6.1: (a) An image with lower part blurred. (b) An image with upper part blurred. (c) Fused image obtained by combining images from (a) and (b) manually. Results of fusion performed by (d) discrete orthogonal wavelet transform (DAUB12), (e) discrete biorthogonal wavelet transform (Bior6.8), and (f) multiscale spline derivative-based transform.

modify wavelet transform coefficients, and Figure 6.2(c) shows the result of enhancement using the multiscale spline derivative-based transform and the same enhancement function as Figure 6.2(b). In this figure, we, more than trying to point out better enhancement results in Figure 6.2(c), observe that Figure 6.2(b) shows features (artifacts) that are not present in the original image (they are particularly obvious in the area right from the mass in Figure 6.2(b)). Here, the goal of enhancement is making visible features that are present in the original image but obstructed by different structures within the same image. Generation of artificial features, while not being rare when nonlinearly processing coefficients of the orthogonal or biorthogonal wavelet transform, is certainly not desirable for this particular application. For more details on different enhancement strategies in mammography, please refer to [11, 22, 23, 25].

Another problem related to enhancement and other kinds of processing of digital mammograms (and not unique to mammography) is that the same mammogram could have been easily translated and/or rotated. From obvious reasons, it is not desirable that the result of processing can be significantly affected by positioning only—one more reason for a translation and rotation-invariant transform.

Figure 6.3 shows outputs from steerable basis filters applied to the image from Figure 6.2(a) at scales $\{1, 2, 4\}$. By linearly combining these outputs analysis along arbitrary direction can be performed (cf. Chapter 4). This enables, as illustrated in Chapter 1, a rotation-invariant processing [21].

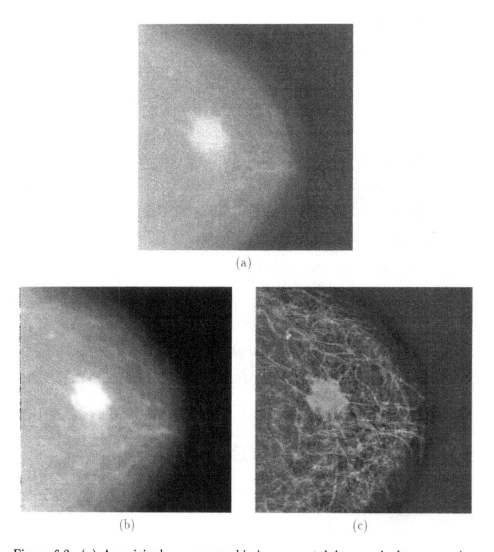

Figure 6.2: (a) An original mammographic image containing a spicular mass. An enhanced image using (b) discrete biorthogonal wavelet transform (Bior6.8) and (c) multiscale spline derivative-based transform.

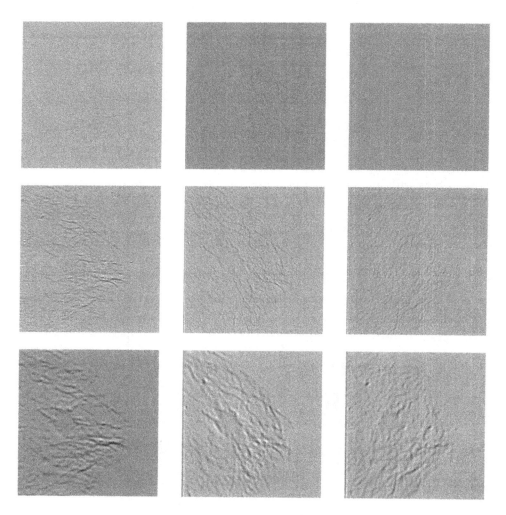

Figure 6.3: The magnitude of filter coefficients for $G_{\Phi}^{\phi_i}(\omega_x, \omega_y)$ at $\phi_i = \{0, \frac{1}{3}\pi, \frac{2}{3}\pi\}$ (three levels of analysis shown).

CHAPTER 7
CONCLUSION

In this thesis we constructed a new transform that does not introduce artifacts due to translation and rotation invariance, which are inherent to traditional wavelet analysis.

We extended the one-dimensional discrete dyadic wavelet transform to higher-order derivatives and even-order spline functions and developed an improved initialization procedure. Comparison to the originally employed initialization [28] showed significantly better performance of our procedure for finer scales of analysis.

We developed several two-dimensional transforms. All of them were derived with the goal of eliminating artifacts due to lack of translation and rotation invariance. We presented a two-dimensional discrete dyadic wavelet transform with a first-derivative wavelet as an extension of the one originally proposed in [28], a two-dimensional discrete dyadic wavelet transform with a second-derivative wavelet that can approximate Laplacian of a Gaussian, and a steerable dyadic wavelet transform implemented in a near-perfect reconstruction filter bank which may be preferred when there is a need for orientation processing along equally spaced angles. We derived a multiscale spline derivative-based transform which uses x-y separable filters in a perfect reconstruction filter bank and enables fast translation and rotation-invariant directional analysis of images.

We empirically showed the presence of artifacts in image fusion and enhancement applications when traditional wavelet methods were used. Here developed transforms did not exhibit similar artifacts, and, in case of fusion, yielded nice results without the use of postprocessing.

66

Future work will concentrate on a more thorough exploitation of the transform space for the existing applications, and potential new applications (e.g., denoising). In particular, we will try to use the causality property of a Gaussian kernel mentioned in Chapter 1 to trace features across scales and process them according to their multiscale behavior.

REFERENCES

[1] A. Aldroubi, M. Unser, and M. Eden, "Cardinal spline filters: Stability and convergence to the ideal sinc interpolator," *Signal Process.*, vol. 28, no. 2, pp. 127–138, 1992.

[2] J. Babaud, A. P. Witkin, M. Baudin, and R. O. Duda, "Uniqueness of the Gaussian kernel for scale-space filtering," *IEEE Trans. Pattern Anal. Mach. Intell.*, vol. 8, no. 1, pp. 26–33, 1986.

[3] C. de Boor, *A Practical Guide to Splines*, Springer-Verlag, New York, NY, 1978.

[4] P. J. Burt and E. H. Adelson, "The Laplacian pyramid as a compact image code," *IEEE Trans. Commun.*, vol. 31, no. 4, pp. 532–540, 1983.

[5] P. J. Burt and R. J. Kolczynski, "Enhanced image capture through fusion," in *Proc. Int. Conf. Comput. Vision*, Berlin, Germany, 1993, pp. 173–182.

[6] J. Canny, "A computational approach to edge detection," *IEEE Trans. Pattern Anal. Mach. Intell.*, vol. 8, no. 6, pp. 679–698, 1986.

[7] L. J. Chipman, T. M. Orr, and L. N. Graham, "Wavelets and image fusion," in *Proc. IEEE Int. Conf. Image Process.*, Washington, D.C., 1995, vol. 3, pp. 248–251.

[8] C. K. Chui, *An Introduction to Wavelets*, Academic Press, San Diego, CA, 1992.

[9] C. K. Chui, Ed., *Wavelets: A Tutorial in Theory and Applications*, Academic Press, San Diego, CA, 1992.

[10] I. Daubechies, *Ten Lectures on Wavelets*, SIAM, Philadelphia, PA, 1992.

[11] J. Fan and A. Laine, "Multiscale contrast enhancement and denoising in digital radiographs," in *Wavelets in Medicine and Biology*, A. Aldroubi and M. Unser, Eds., CRC Press, Boca Raton, FL, 1996, pp. 163–189.

[12] W. T. Freeman and E. H. Adelson, "The design and use of steerable filters," *IEEE Trans. Pattern Anal. Mach. Intell.*, vol. 13, no. 9, pp. 891–906, 1991.

[13] H. Greenspan, S. Belongie, R. Goodman, P. Perona, S. Rakshit, and C. H. Anderson, "Overcomplete steerable pyramid filters and rotation invariance," in *Proc. IEEE Comput. Soc. Conf. Comput. Vision Pattern Recognit.*, Seattle, WA, 1994, pp. 222–228.

[14] Y. Hel-Or and P. C. Teo, "Canonical decomposition of steerable functions," in *Proc. IEEE Comput. Soc. Conf. Comput. Vision Pattern Recognit.*, San Francisco, CA, 1996, pp. 809–816.

[15] M. Holschneider, R. Kronland-Martinet, J. Morlet, and Ph. Tchamitchian, "A real-time algorithm for signal analysis with the help of the wavelet transform," in *Wavelets, Time-Frequency Methods and Phase Space*, J. M. Combes, A. Grossmann, and Ph. Tchamitchian, Eds., Springer-Verlag, Berlin, Germany, 1989, pp. 286–297.

[16] A. J. Jerri, "The Shannon sampling theorem—its various extensions and applications: A tutorial review," *Proc. IEEE*, vol. 65, no. 11, pp. 1565–1596, 1977.

[17] A. Karasaridis and E. Simoncelli, "A filter design technique for steerable pyramid image transforms," in *Proc. IEEE Int. Conf. Acoust. Speech Signal Process.*, Atlanta, GA, 1996, vol. 4, pp. 2389–2392.

[18] I. Koren and A. Laine, "A discrete dyadic wavelet transform for multidimensional feature analysis," in *Time-Frequency and Wavelet Transforms in Biomedical Engineering*, M. Akay, Ed., IEEE Press, New York, NY, 1997.

[19] I. Koren, A. F. Laine, J. Fan, and F. J. Taylor, "Edge detection in echocardiographic image sequences by 3-d multiscale analysis," in *Proc. IEEE Int. Conf. Image Process.*, Austin, TX, 1994, vol. 1, pp. 288–292.

[20] I. Koren, A. Laine, and F. Taylor, "Image fusion using steerable dyadic wavelet transform," in *Proc. IEEE Int. Conf. Image Process.*, Washington, D.C., 1995, vol. 3, pp. 232–235.

[21] I. Koren, A. Laine, F. Taylor, and M. Lewis, "Interactive wavelet processing and techniques applied to digital mammography," in *Proc. IEEE Int. Conf. Acoust. Speech Signal Process.*, Atlanta, GA, 1996, vol. 3, pp. 1415–1418.

[22] A. Laine, J. Fan, and S. Schuler, "A framework for contrast enhancement by dyadic wavelet analysis," in *Digital Mammography*, A. G. Gale, S. M. Astley, D. R. Dance, and A. Y. Cairns, Eds., Elsevier, Amsterdam, The Netherlands, 1994, pp. 91–100.

[23] A. Laine, J. Fan, and W. Yang, "Wavelets for contrast enhancement of digital mammography," *IEEE Eng. Med. Biol. Mag.*, vol. 14, no. 5, pp. 536–550, 1995.

[24] A. Laine, I. Koren, W. Yang, and F. Taylor, "A steerable dyadic wavelet transform and interval wavelets for enhancement of digital mammography," in *Wavelet Applications II*, Proc. SPIE, H. H. Szu, Ed., Orlando, FL, 1995, vol. 2491, pp. 736–749.

[25] A. F. Laine, S. Schuler, J. Fan, and W. Huda, "Mammographic feature enhancement by multiscale analysis," *IEEE Trans. Med. Imaging*, vol. 13, no. 4, pp. 725–740, 1994.

[26] H. Li, B. S. Manjunath, and S. K. Mitra, "Multi-sensor image fusion using the wavelet transform," in *Proc. IEEE Int. Conf. Image Process.*, Austin, TX, 1994, vol. 1, pp. 51–55.

[27] S. Mallat and W. L. Hwang, "Singularity detection and processing with wavelets," *IEEE Trans. Inf. Theory*, vol. 38, no. 2, pp. 617–643, 1992.

[28] S. Mallat and S. Zhong, "Characterization of signals from multiscale edges," *IEEE Trans. Pattern Anal. Mach. Intell.*, vol. 14, no. 7, pp. 710–732, 1992.

[29] D. Marr and E. Hildreth, "Theory of edge detection," *Proc. R. Soc. London Ser. B*, vol. 207, no. 1167, pp. 187–217, 1980.

[30] A. V. Oppenheim and R. W. Schafer, *Discrete-Time Signal Processing*, Prentice-Hall, Englewood Cliffs, NJ, 1989.

[31] P. Perona, "Deformable kernels for early vision," *IEEE Trans. Pattern Anal. Mach. Intell.*, vol. 17, no. 5, pp. 488–499, 1995.

[32] T. Ranchin, L. Wald, and M. Mangolini, "Efficient data fusion using wavelet transform: the case of SPOT satellite images," in *Mathematical Imaging: Wavelet Applications in Signal and Image Processing*, Proc. SPIE, A. F. Laine, Ed., San Diego, CA, 1993, vol. 2034, pp. 171–178.

[33] O. Rioul and P. Duhamel, "Fast algorithms for discrete and continuous wavelet transforms," *IEEE Trans. Inf. Theory*, vol. 38, no. 2, pp. 569–586, 1992.

[34] I. J. Schoenberg, "Contributions to the problem of approximation of equidistant data by analytic functions," *Q. Appl. Math.*, vol. 4, no. 1, pp. 45–99, 112–141, 1946.

[35] I. J. Schoenberg, "Cardinal interpolation and spline functions," *J. Approx. Theory*, vol. 2, no. 2, pp. 167–206, 1969.

[36] I. J. Schoenberg, "Notes on spline functions III: On the convergence of the interpolating cardinal splines as their degree tends to infinity," *Isr. J. Math.*, vol. 16, no. 1, pp. 87–93, 1973.

[37] C. E. Shannon, "Communication in the presence of noise," *Proc. IRE*, vol. 37, no. 1, pp. 10–21, 1949.

[38] E. P. Simoncelli and W. T. Freeman, "The steerable pyramid: A flexible architecture for multi-scale derivative computation," in *Proc. IEEE Int. Conf. Image Process.*, Washington, D.C., 1995, vol. 3, pp. 444–447.

[39] E. P. Simoncelli, W. T. Freeman, E. H. Adelson, and D. J. Heeger, "Shiftable multiscale transforms," *IEEE Trans. Inf. Theory*, vol. 38, no. 2, pp. 587–607, 1992.

[40] M. J. T. Smith and T. P. Barnwell, III, "Exact reconstruction techniques for tree-structured subband coders," *IEEE Trans. Acoust. Speech Signal Process.*, vol. 34, no. 3, pp. 434–441, 1986.

[41] A. Toet, "Image fusion by a ratio of low-pass pyramid," *Pattern Recognit. Lett.*, vol. 9, no. 4, pp. 245–253, 1989.

[42] M. Unser and A. Aldroubi, "A general sampling theory for nonideal acquisition devices," *IEEE Trans. Signal Process.*, vol. 42, no. 11, pp. 2915–2925, 1994.

[43] M. Unser, A. Aldroubi, and M. Eden, "Fast B-spline transforms for continuous image representation and interpolation," *IEEE Trans. Pattern Anal. Mach. Intell.*, vol. 13, no. 3, pp. 277–285, 1991.

[44] M. Unser, A. Aldroubi, and M. Eden, "On the asymptotic convergence of B-spline wavelets to Gabor functions," *IEEE Trans. Inf. Theory*, vol. 38, no. 2, pp. 864–872, 1992.

[45] M. Unser, A. Aldroubi, and M. Eden, "Polynomial spline signal approximations: Filter design and asymptotic equivalence with Shannon's sampling theorem," *IEEE Trans. Inf. Theory*, vol. 38, no. 1, pp. 95–103, 1992.

[46] M. Unser, A. Aldroubi, and S. J. Schiff, "Fast implementation of the continuous wavelet transform with integer scales," *IEEE Trans. Signal Process.*, vol. 42, no. 12, pp. 3519–3523, 1994.

[47] M. Vrhel, C. Lee, and M. Unser, "Fast computation of the continuous wavelet transform through oblique projections," in *Proc. IEEE Int. Conf. Acoust. Speech Signal Process.*, Atlanta, GA, 1996, vol. 3, pp. 1459–1462.

[48] A. Witkin, "Scale space filtering," in *Proc. Int. Joint Conf. Artif. Intell.*, Karlsruhe, Germany, 1983, pp. 1019–1022.

BIOGRAPHICAL SKETCH

Iztok Koren earned the B.S. and M.S. degrees in electrical engineering from the University of Ljubljana, Slovenia, in 1987 and 1991, respectively. He will receive the Ph.D. degree in electrical and computer engineering from the University of Florida, Gainesville, in 1996.

His research interests include image processing, digital signal processing, and wavelets.

He is a member of Eta Kappa Nu, Tau Beta Pi, and the IEEE.

I certify that I have read this study and that in my opinion it conforms to acceptable standards of scholarly presentation and is fully adequate, in scope and quality, as a dissertation for the degree of Doctor of Philosophy.

Fred J. Taylor, Chairman
Professor of Electrical and Computer
Engineering

I certify that I have read this study and that in my opinion it conforms to acceptable standards of scholarly presentation and is fully adequate, in scope and quality, as a dissertation for the degree of Doctor of Philosophy.

Andrew F. Laine , Cochairman
Associate Professor of Computer and
Information Science and Engineering

I certify that I have read this study and that in my opinion it conforms to acceptable standards of scholarly presentation and is fully adequate, in scope and quality, as a dissertation for the degree of Doctor of Philosophy.

Jose C. Principe
Professor of Electrical and Computer
Engineering

I certify that I have read this study and that in my opinion it conforms to acceptable standards of scholarly presentation and is fully adequate, in scope and quality, as a dissertation for the degree of Doctor of Philosophy.

John M. M. Anderson
Assistant Professor of Electrical and
Computer Engineering

I certify that I have read this study and that in my opinion it conforms to acceptable standards of scholarly presentation and is fully adequate, in scope and quality, as a dissertation for the degree of Doctor of Philosophy.

Kermit Sigmon
Associate Professor of Mathematics

This dissertation was submitted to the Graduate Faculty of the College of Engineering and to the Graduate School and was accepted as partial fulfillment of the requirements for the degree of Doctor of Philosophy.

December 1996

Winfred M. Phillips
Dean, College of Engineering

Karen A. Holbrook
Dean, Graduate School

www.ingramcontent.com/pod-product-compliance
Lightning Source LLC
Chambersburg PA
CBHW060457060326
40689CB00020B/4560